Teen Resources On the Web

A Guide for Librarians, Parents and Teachers

Mimi Mandel

Alleyside Press®

Fort Atkinson, Wisconsin

Published by Alleyside Press,
an imprint of Highsmith Press LLC
Highsmith Press
W5527 Highway 106
P.O. Box 800
Fort Atkinson, Wisconsin 53538-0800
1-800-558-2110

The paper used in this publication meets the minimum
requirements of the American National Standard for
Information Science - Permanence of Paper for Printed
Library Material. ANSI/NISO Z39.48-1992.

Library of Congress Cataloging-in-Publication Data

Mandel, Mimi.
   Teen resources on the web : a guide for librarians, parents
and teachers / Mimi Mandel.
        p. cm.
Includes index.
   ISBN 1-57950-042-0 (pb : acid-free)
 1. Teenagers--Computer network resources.
2. Teenagers. 3. Web sites--Directories. I. Title.
   HQ796 .M248 2000
   025.04--dc21
                         00-008356

Contents

Link www.hpress.highsmith.com/mmup.htm

Introduction

The World Wide Web can be a fascinating wonderland filled with a wealth of information, activities and opportunities. Or it can be a frustrating wasteland plagued by traffic jams, circuitous detours and dead ends. The *Teen Guide* will help make teens' journeys on the Web more rewarding than rambling. Thousands upon thousands of difficult-to-use, slow-loading or information-weak sites were pored over to find the selection listed in this guide. Not only have we culled user-friendly, professionally produced and content-packed websites, we have assembled only sites on topics of interest to teens.

How the Guide Is Organized

The information in the chapters and appendices of the *Teens Guide* encompasses aspects of everything a teen needs to know to have a productive journey in cyberspace. In chapter one, Wonders of the Web, there is a review of the fundamentals of e-mail, newsgroups and mailing lists, and chat rooms. Chapter two, How to Find Anything on the World Wide Web, provides tips for effective searching to enable teens to find what they need, when they need it, not after hours and hours of frustration. In the Reference Resources, beginning on page 11, there are over 900 cherry-picked websites that range in topic from Activism to Writing and everything in between.

Each description includes a brief review of the website, specific highlights, URL, source or authority, and how it can help the teenager. Any special features, such as the ability to e-mail your local senator or download free shareware, are also mentioned. Reading the reviews before logging on will help focus the time spent online.

Three appendices follow the main body. The first two give brief pointers on netiquette and safe Web behaviors. The third, a handy reference for college bound teens, is a list of over 900 colleges in the U.S. with their URLs. And finally, there is an index of websites by site name at the end of the *Guide*.

Subject Coverage

Teens have wide-ranging interests, and we have tried to include sites that will connect them with information they want and need. From lifelong learning sources to entertainment and leisure—there is a little something for every teen. Need to know what kind of weather to expect at that outdoor concert? Or what to do with that new stock your teen just bought with babysitting money? Get instant stock quotes, weather forecasts and up to the minute global news from the Web. Tour a museum that happens to be located on the other side of the planet, chat in real time with a famous celebrity, and download music clips from the hottest band. And while there are lots of music, chat, sports and entertainment sites in the *Guide*, careful attention has also been given to sites teens might need for homework or life planning.

In the reference area, teens will have access to vast holdings, including abstracts of articles and sometimes even full-text books online. They can review historic manuscripts or practice speaking and hearing almost any language. Ask-an-Expert websites answer questions that run the gamut from "what to do with my acne" to a daunting calculus problem. Historians, educators, inventors, writers, mathematicians, you name it—from any field, are publishing and exchanging their ideas online. What does this mean to teens? It means that with the click of a few buttons, they can access the latest information about 3D animation or cutting edge inventions. Writing research papers just got a whole lot easier. With the Web resources now available and help in finding the most useful ones—in history, math, science and literature—the information and resources students need to compete in today's changing environment are literally at their fingertips.

Teens interested in researching health issues can access medical journals, learn about pharmaceuticals, drug interactions, see pictures of the human body and even watch physicians perform live surgery. Students interested in political activities can find a host of websites about politics. Almost every governmental agency has a website with information about its programs. Budding entrepreneurs can even start their own businesses quite inexpensively by opening a storefront on the Web, selling merchandise at dozens of Web auctions or classified ad sites.

In addition to providing tremendous reference resources, the Web also offers an extensive range of courses, lesson plans and tutorials. Searchers can sign up for any of the thousands of courses given by experts, training institutes, and colleges. Teens can take courses that may not be offered in their area or for a subject not offered at their institution.

A large section of the *Teen Guide* is devoted to college life, college planning, college search and college admissions. Students don't even have to leave their home to go through the entire planning, searching and application process. The Internet offers virtual tours of college campuses designed to familiarize the prospective applicant with the campus. Some websites have the capability to deliver a student's college application package via e-mail to as many as 50 colleges at one time. A number of sites publish exemplary college application essays with online help. Information on financial aid for college is contained on many sites, and we have included some of the best resources. And finally, on page 103, the alphabetical list of over 900 URLs for colleges and universities all around the country.

Sites selected are graphically engaging and easy to use. Most have hyperlinks to photographs, video clips, audio clips, primary source documents, and lists of other pertinent links. Many sites also invite teens to submit their work for Web publication, including artwork, poet-ry, videos, photographs, and writing.

Only you and your teen's imagination limit the diversity of information and experiences available on the Internet. Whether taking a virtual tour of their first choice college, researching for that report that is 33 percent of their grade, checking out current football scores, or experimenting with new hairstyles, this guide ensures that you can recommend a wealth of interesting and safe sites appropriate for teens to explore online.

Staying Current

Although the World Wide Web is a wonderful resource, obsolescence is an issue. The addresses, or Uniform Resource Locators (URLs), of the websites are constantly changing. Websites are terminated or replaced everyday. To extend the usefulness of the *Teen Guide*, changes to the websites will be posted on a page designated for this purpose (http://www.hpress.highsmith.com/mmup.htm). If you should experience any problem in using this special feature, or discover a URL that no longer functions, please send an e-mail to hpress@highsmith.com.

Chapter 1

The Wonders of the Web

E-mail

Electronic mail, referred to as e-mail, has quickly become the most effective and popular way to communicate. Instead of writing a letter, applying a stamp and taking it to a mailbox or post office, you can now send letters digitally in seconds for free. As long as the other party has an e-mail address, you can exchange messages. You can also send any file, web page, music clip, audio clip, manuscript, photograph or letter. If it's stored in your computer or can be scanned into your computer, it can be e-mailed.

In order to use e-mail you need a computer, of course and a valid e-mail account. Free e-mail accounts are available from a number of websites such as:

http://www.yahoo.com

http://www.hotmail.com

http://www.juno.com

Newsgroups and Mailing Lists

Newsgroups and Mailing Lists are forums people can join to discuss topics of interest. After subscribing to a mailing list, it will come to your e-mail address either in single messages or in a digest form (where all messages for the day are grouped together. You can simply read the messages, and then post or send messages on that topic.

Newsgroups and Mailing Lists represent a diversity of lifestyles, religions, and cultures. Read through mailing lists and newsgroups before you post anything. This helps you to get an understanding of the nature (or culture) of the group.

Tips for successful participation in Newsgroups and Mailing Lists:

- Messages and articles should be brief and to the point.

- Try not to wander off-topic, ramble or post unintelligible information.

- Generally, it is considered poor netiquette to advertise products or services.

- Save the welcome messages you will receive when you join a group. At some point you may want to know how to unsubscribe from the group.

- Before hitting "send," be certain you really want the message to go just as you have written it. Once it has been sent, you cannot get it back.

- When you cannot check your mail for an extended period, set the "nomail" option so you don't get bombarded with mail when you finally return.

- Never assume that any information you find is up-to-date and/or true. The Internet enables anyone to be a publisher, but not everyone understands their responsibilities.

- When you reply to a post, summarize the original so that others understand when they read your response.

- Be careful when you reply to messages. Sometimes a reply is sent back to the address it came from, usually the address of a group. You may accidentally send a personal response to a great many people, wasting their time and space, or even worse, embarrassing them or yourself. To avoid this, type in the address instead of relying on "reply." Get into the habit of double checking the address before you click "send."

- If you accidentally send a personal message to the whole group, send an apology to the person and to the group.

- Don't get involved in flame wars (messages criticizing others). Neither post nor respond to inflammatory material.

- Avoid sending messages that are replies to replies.

- Do not betray confidences. It is all too easy to quote a personal letter in a posting to the entire group.

- Treat every post as though you were sending a copy to your boss, your minister, and a member of your favorite college's admissions committee.

- Remember your tone of voice cannot be heard. Use emoticons or smilies, i.e., (-: or)-:

- Sexually and racially harassing messages are illegal and immoral.

- Curse words will often get you bounced or even permanently banned from a group.

Chat Rooms

The World Wide Web lets you communicate with other people live in real time in chat rooms. Chat rooms have been developed for every type of individual, interest, profession and subject.

General advice for positive chat experiences:

- It is not necessary to greet everyone on a channel or room personally.

- Don't assume that people will want to talk to you.

- If a chatter is using a nickname alias or pseudonym, respect their anonymity.

Chapter 2

How to Find Anything on the World Wide Web

Tips for Effective Searching

Nobody likes to sit and stare at the computer while waiting for information to be delivered. Equally frustrating is the process of searching for specific information and never finding it. The Internet contains over 300 million documents, and this number is doubling every six to twelve months. The only problem is: how do you find what you want? To find information quickly, you must select the right keyword. Every search engine has a place for you to type words that describe what you're seeking. Search engines are programmed to match your query words, called keywords, with the words in its databases. It then feeds back to you a list of sites that share those words. It is imperative that the keywords are precise, since a computer cannot reason like a human brain and it is generally unable to interpret subtleties. Computers are dependent upon humans to draft the right questions. Poor queries give poor results. Good queries give good results.

Wouldn't it be great if there was one gigantic online search engine that had a database of the entire contents of the Internet? Unfortunately, it doesn't exist. Every search engine, (and there are hundreds) uses different search techniques and various software tools (called spiders) to build indexes of the Internet. When doing searches through them, they also show different "views" of the web.

Topic Specific Search Engines

With over one thousand online search engines, selecting an engine that specializes in a specific topic is very helpful. Some engines contain databases that are designed for specific groups only with sites for education or children or even for the novice. Here are examples of several topic specific search engines:

Yahooligans http://www.yahooligans
A search engine for children's sites

Simple Search.com http://www.SimpleSearch.com
Targeted for the new computer user.

EuroFerret http://www.euroferret.com/
Contains 35 million European websites

Music Search http://musicsearch.com/
Thousands of music-related sites.

Hierarchical Search Engines

Search engines use different search techniques. The type that shows different "views" of the Web is called a 'hierarchical' search engine. It is based on subjects like lists of auctions or manufacturers of ski boots. The ever-popular Yahoo is an example of a hierarchical directory where the subjects are broken down from large subjects to smaller categories within the bigger topic. Here are examples of the directory type of search engine:

AltaVista http://www.altavista.digital.com
Excite http://www.excite.com
Hotbot http://www.hotbot.com
Infoseek http://www.infoseek.com
Lycos http://www.lycos.com
Magellan http://www.mckinley.com
Northern Light http://www.nlsearch.com
WebCrawler http://www.webcrawler.com

Key Word Search Engines

The other type of search engines stores the information according to words or terms. Here are some examples:

LookSmart http://www.looksmart.com
Mining Company http://home.miningco.com

Meta Search Engines

Wouldn't it be convenient if you could search more that one engine at the same time? Somebody beat you to that idea! Many search engines search ten, twenty or even more engines at once. Appropriately called metasearchers, some are:

Metacrawler http://www.metacrawler.com

Inference http://www.inference.com/infind/

SavvySearch
  http://guaraldi.cs.colostate.edu:2000/

After clicking on a search engine, read the tool's description, search options, and rules and restrictions before trying to perform a search. You want to use the most precise query as possible. Words that are commonly used like "the," "and," and "of" make poor search keywords. Just leave them out. Articles and prepositions are ignored completely. Strive for words that highlight the differences between information sources. The more distinctive a word, the sharper your search and the answers will be closer to what you need.

Make a habit of using more than one search engine. You will develop an understanding of the idiosyncrasies of each engine and begin to know which is the best for each topic. The kind of information a database contains can have dramatic effects on the search process. A particular keyword phrase may work perfectly well on one index, and poorly on another. With experience, you will develop intuition about which keywords to use with each engine.

Common Problems

What if my search produces no results?
Is it spelled right? Did you read the description of the search engine that tells you how it works? Not all search tools are created equal. Have you over-simplified? If you are searching for information about a specific rock and roll band, just using the words "rock and roll" may not be specific enough. Have you tried a synonym or variations on words?

What if my search produces too many results?
Be more specific. Instead of "rock and roll", name the specific band or artists. Try to think of words that uniquely identify what you're looking for. Some words are of little value, because they identify lots of documents. The more distinctive a word, the more useful it will be for sharpening your search. Try to use as many relevant keywords as possible; it will help to uniquely identify what you're looking for.

What if I don't get an answer or the server is too busy?
The server you are trying to access may be too busy or temporarily down. Try again in a few minutes. Wait until a less busy time of the day. Avoid prime time hours when everybody and their sister are trying to go online.

What if Error 404, (Page/File not found) appears?
It is possible that the link no longer exists, that the URL has been changed or is simply no longer valid. Double check your URL, make sure it's correct. Check the lower/upper case of each character. URLs are partially case-sensitive. The first part, the domain name is NOT case sensitive, but everything that follows after the net, org or edu IS (i.e., /path.../filename). If your URL has more than one directory level, try to move up in the tree (i.e., remove the last level and try again).
For example:

http://www.exploratorium.com/learning_studio /index.html,

If you were unsuccessful at this level, delete the learning_studio/index.html, and you will probably get the main site at http://www.exploratorium.

What if it says permission denied?
That site may deny public access. Not all sites are free and open to the public. Try again later. Sometimes the restricted access is only for a certain period of the day. Sometimes a site will require that you register, get a password or subscribe.

Chapter 3

Reference Resources

Activism (*See also* Voluntarism)

Act as if what you do makes a difference.
It does. – William James

All Stars Helping Kids

http://www.allstars.kids.org/

Founded in 1989 by NFL great Ronnie Lott, All Stars Helping Kids is non-profit organization founded on the concept that "it takes a village" to raise a child. Through benefits and special events, money is raised to fund organizations that focus on disadvantaged youth. This site highlights the work of groups that often are the best hope for children facing the reality of disabilities, family problems, crime and economic hardship. The most visible volunteers of All Stars Helping Kids are, of course, the celebrity athletes. But other volunteers are just as special. Teens who are interested can click here to learn more.

Bread for the World

http://www.bread.org/

Bread for the World hosts an international Christian activist organization dedicated to relieving the plight of the impoverished. Features include Action Alert, Guide to Congress, Jobs/Internships, and Journalist Resources. Get Ending Hunger e-news free to find out what you can do to fight world hunger.

Civicus

http://www.civicus.org/

With the loftiest goal around of uniting the world, Civicus offers many programs, publications, projects, and information on harmoniously bringing together political, economic, and cultural life—especially in areas where democracy and freedom of citizens are threatened.

Connect for Kids

http://www.connectforkids.org/

A virtual encyclopedia of information for adults who want to make their communities better places for kids. Through radio, print, and TV ads, a weekly e-mail newsletter, and a discussion forum, this award-winning project provides the tools to help people become more active citizens—from volunteering to voting—on behalf of kids. Sponsored by the Benton Foundation.

CyberActivist

http://www.cyberhomepage.com/cybercnn.htm

Complex in intent and structure (with three active frames), the CyberActivist Control Panel offers a companion to CNN's daily programming. This site contains the CyberActivist Tool Kit which is intended to empower citizens worldwide to take control of important issues. The CyberActivist Control Panel seeks to convert TV news viewing from the passive to the interactive. Everyone around the world can be linked to more than 15,000 governmental officials worldwide as well as 2,000 media outlets.

The Electronic Activist

http://www.berkshire.net/~ifas/activist/

Want to change the world? How about your state? Something wrong in your own community you want the people who make the laws to know about? You can make a difference! One of the ways you can bring about change is by writing to your lawmakers. It has never been easier. This site is an e-mail address directory of congress people, state governments, and media entities.

Impact Online

http://www.impactonline.org/

For students looking to get involved: Whether it's building a house for Habitat for Humanity, organizing an arts and crafts fair for inner-city children, or participating in an AIDS walk-a-thon, this nonprofit organization can find the perfect volunteer opportunity to fit everyone's interests and schedules. Sponsored by Impact Online, Incorporated. This is a free online matching service for volunteers and nonprofits.

Peace Resource Center

http://www1.umn.edu/humanrts/peace/

The Peace Resource Center contains a search engine that specializes in searching the Web for information relating to peace and human rights information. It also has lists of General Peace Documents, War and Peace

Documents, Recent Peace Accords, Humanitarian Law, International Criminal Tribunals, Peace & Activist Links, and Public Awareness sections. Sponsored by the University of Minnesota Human Rights Center.

Proactivist

http://www.proactivist.com/index1.html

This site photographically documents protests and demonstrations. Its goal is to assist young activists. View the calendar of upcoming events, an extensive index of links, a bulletin board for exchanging thoughts and ideas, RealAudio recordings from protests, and tips on how to run an effective event.

Stolen Dreams

http://www.hsph.harvard.edu/gallery/intro.html

Sponsored by the Harvard School of Public Health, this site contains a gallery of photographs taken by David Parker, MD, of children working in a variety of occupations in the United States, Mexico, Thailand, Nepal, Bangladesh, Turkey, Morocco, Indonesia, and India. You will see young children working in dangerous and unsanitary conditions in developing nations.

Student School Change Network

http://www.nmia.com/~sscn/

A slightly radical yet thought-provoking organization. Dedicated to changing the focus of education, SSCN wants students and teachers from high schools across the country to unite behind a curriculum tailored to the students' point of view. Offers a free student-power handbook with additional information.

Web Directory: Internet Resources on Child Labor

http://www.natlconsumersleague.org/kidlabur.htm

The National Consumers League has put together a comprehensive list of sites on the Internet devoted to child labor. There are governmental organizations, international organizations, student groups, advocacy groups and campaigns. NCL is a private, nonprofit membership organization dedicated to representing consumers on issues of concern to consumers.

Youth in Action

http://www.mightymedia.com/youth/

An interactive online service that brings together youth and educators around the world to learn about, and participate in, positive social action and service projects — from the environment to human rights. A free registration process is required for access to the programs. Sponsored by Mighty Media.

YouthSpeak

http://www.oblivion.net/youthspeak/

YouthSpeak is a grassroots citizen organization working to empower youth and allow youth to make the democratic choices that affect their lives through voting. YouthSpeak is the only nationwide organization whose sole purpose is to allow youth the right to vote. Sponsored by Youth Speak.

Advice

Not all those who wander are lost. – J.R.R. Tolkien

(Because of the variety of information that may be found on these websites, parents, teachers and librarians may wish to visit these sites before referring teens to them.)

Ask Annie

http://members.tripod.com/~biopharm/askannie.htm

For the many teens who have problems, but are too unsure or embarrassed to talk with the people they see every day. Ask Annie lets them talk with someone their own age, who understands what they're going through. It's the truthfulness, helpfulness, and been-there, know-what-you-mean.

Kitana's Advice for Teens

http://www.angelfire.com/ca/freeadvice4teens/

Yahoo's #1 site for advice for teens is one place to send students who are looking for a fresh viewpoint. They can ask Kitana about parents, friends, school, or whatever happens to be on their mind—through e-mail or in a live chat room.

Teen Advice

http://www.teenadvice.org/

Not just for teens, Teen Advice Online is always on call to help parents, teachers, and, yep, even teens with any teenage problem around.

Teen Talk

http://www.teentalk.com/

Sometimes, teens need advice from anyone and everyone. That's when they should come here to Teen Talk. This teen advice site lets them post their problems and e-mail address, letting anyone who happens to see it respond with helpful guidance.

Time Warp Advice

http://www.MissAbigail.com/

A funny collection of books, spanning from 1832 to 1977, that covers the age-old topics of dating, love, living together, puberty, marriage, sex, etiquette, housekeeping, and even home repairs. Step back in time with quotes, tidbits, and words of wisdom to help with today's dilemmas.

Alcoholism (*See* Substance Abuse)

Animals (*See also* Science--Life Sciences)

Cats are smarter than dogs. You cannot get eight cats to pull a sled through snow. – Jeff Valdez

All About Cats

http://w3.one.net/~mich/

All About Cats is all about cats! Download pictures of cats from all over the net, win cat prizes by taking a cat quiz, and get cat advice at the cat advice column.

Dog & Kennel

http://www.dogandkennel.com

The comprehensive, authoritative, and enlightening guide to all you every wanted to know about the world of dogs.

The Electronic Zoo

http://netvet.wustl.edu/e-zoo.htm

What started out as a medical resource for veterinarians back in 1995, is now a thorough collection of links to other animal websites. Each week they introduce "what's new" in the animal world. A search engine allows users to type any keyword relating to animals and veterinary medicine and a list of matching sites will appear.

Flights of Fancy

http://home.earthlink.net/~edwardsjm/jme.index.html

Birds, bugs, and beetles. A very attractive site devoted to birds, conservation, ecology and a multitude of planet earth-related topics.

Habitat for Horses, Inc.

http://www.habitatforhorses.org/

A nonprofit organization that rescues abused, endangered horses, giving them a lifetime home with all the health and psychological care they need. Read about their programs, stories, see photographs and learn how to adopt a horse.

Pet Dir

http://www.PetDir.com/petdir/top.html

An extensive directory of pets and everything pertaining to pets. Under the Dog section, they don't just offer boarding, breeding and bedding information, but also topics like odor control, sitters and clubs. Animated graphics make this site fun to visit and the content will keep animal lovers busy for hours.

Petlinks.com

http://24.28.86.225/petlinks/

A comprehensive listing of every imaginable family pet you might own and then some you thought nobody would own. From arachnids to chinchillas to marsupials to wallabies, this site contains terrific information on a wide variety of pets. For each animal, Petlinks gives a description of the pet and then provides more links for that specific animal.

Art

What is art but a way of seeing? – Thomas Berger

Art Crimes: The Writing on the Wall

http://www.graffiti.org/

See a side of art that most mistake for gang crime: graffiti. This Internet gallery celebrates graffiti art, providing cultural information and resources to help preserve and document this constantly changing and disappearing art form. Includes more than 2,000 images from more than 80 cities worldwide.

Art on the Net

http://www.artonthenet.net/

Art on the Net hosts its own original gallery and connects the user to other virtual galleries and exhibits. It also features a compilation of links to art magazines and journals, and art schools.

Clip-Art.com

http://www.clip-art.com/

Clip-Art.com presents a colorful palette of free, downloadable images and graphics. Thousands of eye-catching icons are organized into searchable archives arranged by theme; special sections offer animated dividers, backgrounds, and more.

HypArt

http://www.work.de/cgi-bin/HypArt.sh

A site where students are the artists. Here, art is taken to the digital age by collecting individual computer-generated pieces of art and connecting them together on the Web—making a single picture created by several people. Anyone can submit a piece and everyone is welcome to view the current one being created — or to browse the gallery of completed projects. Sponsored by Klaus Rosenfeld.

International Directory of Art Libraries

http://iberia.vassar.edu/ifla-idal/

This online directory contains nearly 3,000 libraries with specialized holdings in art, architecture, and archaeology throughout the world. To search this resource, users can enter any distinctive word or phrase. The current address of each institution will be listed.

The Metropolitan Museum of Art

http://www.metmuseum.org/home.asp

The Metropolitan is one of the largest and finest art museums in the world. Its collections include more than two million works of art — several hundred thousand of which are on view at any given time — spanning more than 5,000 years of world culture, from prehistory to the present. Students who visit the site will have multiple options, ranging from tours, reading the latest museum news, obtaining membership information, visiting the museum shop, and much more.

MoMA: The Museum of Modern Art (New York)

http://www.moma.org/

This full-featured site will appeal to everyone from young students to adults. It includes information on current and future exhibits, images from the collection and details of film, video and other museum programs. This site has won many significant awards for the quality and variety of its content, which will enrich the art aficionado, student, teacher, or anyone who appreciates the arts.

Museum of Fine Arts (Boston, Mass.)

http://www.mfa.org/

Directing teens to this website will give them the opportunity to experience one of the better museum-related sites on the Internet. They'll discover some of the museum's great works of art through an online tour, and learn about its most popular objects and special exhibits.

The National Gallery (London)

http://www.nationalgallery.org.uk/

The National Gallery in London houses one of the world's finest collections of Western European paintings, over 2,300 works completed between 1270 and 1900. The museum website can provide information about its collections, exhibitions, lecture schedule, news releases or general information. It even offers a game that would be of special interest to young people.

The National Gallery of Art (Washington, DC)

http://www.nga.gov

The site for this world class museum contains a database of information on all of the more than 100,000 objects in the collection. Much of the art can be viewed online with PDF guides included. In-depth study tours are available here on a number of artists.

Royal London Wax Museum

http://www.waxworld.com/

Not too many wax museums in the world compare with this one, which is located in Victoria, British Colombia. It may not be in the easiest place to visit, but thanks to the Internet, this site will offer students a world of information about wax creations. Visitors can obtain a "Cook's tour" of the exhibits, and learn about the history of wax sculpture.

Teens Only Computer Art Gallery

http://members.aol.com/pmccoy505/teen/art.htm

Grandma Moses may have started creating art when she was a senior citizen, but that doesn't mean teenagers need to wait that long. This teen-only art museum is a great venue for up-and-coming teen artists to submit and display their works of art, whether it is created on the computer or just transferred there, for the world to see and critique.

Yahoo's List of Art Museums

http://dir.yahoo.com/Arts/Museums__Galleries__ and_Centers/

The Yahoo directory of art museums and galleries provides a collection of hyperlinks to international art and art history resources. Links are listed alphabetically and categorized by resource type.

WWW Art Guide

http://www.artcents.com/artguide/

The WWW Art Guide provides a keyword-searchable database of thousands of art resources on the Web. Well-organized and cross-referenced into browsable artist, art schools, museums, dance, digital art, art supplies, instructors, and associations.

World Wide Arts Resources

http://www.world-arts-resources.com/northameria
 _museums.html

Art students and teachers can access almost all the online art museums in the world through this site. They can browse by location or alphabetically by name or subject. If visitors do not want to browse the categories, the site features a search engine that enables them to quickly search through over 150,000 arts pages.

Automobiles (*See also* Driver Education)

Sometimes it's a little better to travel than to arrive.
 – Zen and the Art of Motorcycle Maintenance

AutoWeb.com

http://www.autoweb.com/

Whether your teens are researching information on their first car, or they're looking for that well-needed trade up, there's no better place to cruise. This site offers information on buying a new or used car, or selling your own car, plus additional information on financing, insurance and maintenance.

Cartalk.com

http://www.cartalk.com

Can't wait to drive? Need a car? Got a car? Wanna sell a car? Fix a car? Then you've come to the right place. Tom and Ray Magliozzi (aka "Click and Clack, The Tappet Brothers") have a weekly show on 450 National Public Radio stations, and a newspaper column in 300 papers. America's funniest auto mechanics, they are "the Marx Brothers meet Mr. Goodwrench." To learn from these M.I.T.-educated grease monkeys, check out their site.

Biography

Never confuse motion with action.
 –Ernest Hemingway

African American Resources

http://dewey.chs.chico.k12.ca.us/afri.html

Students will not find any fancy graphics or even any pictures at this site, just a comprehensive list of links to Black History resources on the Internet. Young surfers will find biographies of African Americans who have contributed to the advancement of science and engineering, literature, film, politics, and the perspectives of Black women, among other aspects of African American culture. Sponsored by Chico High School Library.

Biographical Dictionary

www.s9.com/biography

This dictionary covers more than 28,000 notable men and women who have made important contributions to the world from ancient times to the present day. While the entries are brief, there is a tremendous selection. The dictionary can be searched by birth years, death years, positions held, professions, literary and artistic works, achievements, and other keywords.

Biography.com

http://www.biography.com

Watch 2500 videos and read about 25,000 personalities in this biography mega-site. Features "Born on This Day" and "This Day in History." From athletes to world leaders, almost anyone of any notoriety can be found here.

Distinguished Women of Past and Present

http://www.DistinguishedWomen.com/

This site contains biographies of women who made contributions to American culture. Biographies of writers, educators, scientists, heads of state, politicians, civil rights crusaders, artists, entertainers, and others are included. Whether they lived hundreds of years ago and are still living today, there are many fascinating figures represented here. Many of the names will be known, but many more have been ignored by history book writers

Famous Hispanics in the World and History

http://coloquio.com/famosos/alpha.html

A barebones listing of over 200 short biographies of famous Hispanics. The main page is dedicated to celebrating Hispanic heritage in the United States and elsewhere in the world.

Find a Grave

http://www.findagrave.com/

A database of over 2.5 million records of graves. Search by name. Location, claim to fame, and birth and death dates.

Gallery of Achievers

http://www.achievement.org/galleryachieve.html

The Gallery of Achievers focuses on individuals who have shaped the twentieth century through their accomplishments. Biographies, profiles and interviews provide a closer look at the lives of these American figures with the intent that their experiences will motivate and educate others. These contemporary role models have been drawn from many walks of life: the Arts, Public Service, Sports, Business and Science and Exploration.

PBS History, Biographies

www.pbs.org/history/bios.html

Not a large listing of biographies, but some notables included such as Buckminster Fuller, General MacArthur, and Theodore Roosevelt. The main site features companion guides for PBS's many educational television programs such as *Nova*'s "Ice Mummies of the Inca" and the "Lost Tribes of Israel."

Best of the Web

The best things in life aren't things.   – Art Buchwald

Best of the Planet Awards

http://www.2ask.com/

Want to know the secrets of the search engines? Or, its 2 a.m. and you've got a research paper due at 9:00 a.m., and you cannot find anything anywhere about the natural habitats of the Aborigines of Australia. Here's the place to look! We'll give you a clue. Two things will help you find the right information. Proper keyword selection is important but so is choosing the right search engine.

Cool Central

http://www.coolcentral.com/

This features the Cool Site of the Week, the Cool Site of the Day, the Cool Site of the Hour, and, for teens in a real hurry, the Cool Site of the Moment.

Free Launch

http://www.freelaunch.com/

Don't let anyone tell you there's no such things as a "Free Launch." This collection of websites does not quite fall into the hotlist category, but they are not quite index level either. These sites were chosen for their "enduring bookmark value" as the webmasters immodestly boast. Since they have been at it awhile, you will find many quality listings archived from past years.

Internet Plaza

http://1-internetplaza.com/

This site claims to only list the BEST sites on the Web. Categories include: Kids (toys, videos, stuffed animals), Gifts (candles, food, jewelry, clothes), Sports (skateboarding, inline skating, snowboarding, bowling, scuba diving, apparel), Hobbies (model rockets, plastic models, model trains), Household (pets, decorations, furnishings), Fashion (clothing, sportswear, jewelry), Business Services and Religion.

Over the Edge Award of Excellence

http://www.camelotdesign.com/winaward.htm

This website gives awards to outstanding sites. Your teens can submit their favorite site or just enjoy the many award winners that are listed here. In the Winners Circle viewers will find listings in Art, Literature, Music, Multimedia, Webmasters, Graphics,and many other Web resources.

PC Magazine's Top 100 Web Sites

http://www.zdnet.com/pcmag/special/web100/

From the publishers at ZDNet, who produce PC Magazine Online, Yahoo!, Internet Life, and a host of other great magazines, this site lists 100 of the Web's Best. The five categories are Commerce, Computing, Entertainment, News & Views, and Reference. Covers everything from online stores to computing resources with some entertainment sites sprinkled in for fun.

Project Cool Sighting

http://www.projectcool.com/sightings/

Features a daily sighting of the best sites. Check out their archive of past best sites. If your teens know of an example of a truly great website, here's the chance to submit it for consideration. Looking over the archives provides some amazing lessons in Web design.

Teen Hoopla: An Internet Guide for Teens

http://www.ala.org/teenhoopla

More of the best for teens, this time selected by members of the Young Adult Library Services Asson. Subject areas include Arts and Entertainment, Books, Homework, Internet, Sports and more.

Top 50 Sites That Download Quickly

http://www.zazz.com/fast50/index.shtml

Don't have a Sun workstation, cable modem, and a T3 connection to the Internet? Your teen could have the most ancient, obsolete, slowest connection but these sites will still download fast. This collection represents the fastest sites on the Web.

Top 1%

http://www.web-search.com/cool.html

What if your teens could remove all of the boring, irrelevant, unimportant stuff you find that clutters search engines and keep the cool stuff? This search engine is devoted to subjects like Comedy, Music, Magazines, Shopping, Travel, Chat, E-mail, Sports, Photography, Personal Ads, etc. Sound like it was custom tailored just for teens?

Top Ten Sites

http://www.toptensites.com

Each contributor provides the top ten sites in their subject area. The lists are updated weekly so you have access to the newest best sites available. With categories like Guitar, Games, and Relationships, this is a top ten list sure to interest teens.

Weekly Hot 100 Websites

http://www.100hot.com/

This is a search engine with a slightly different twist. It covers all the same categories as the other big search engines, but the unique aspect is that it selects the Top 100 for almost everything, such as the 100 hot sports sites, the 100 hot travel sites, and the 100 hot joke sites.

Wow! Web Wonders

http://www.bergen.org/AAST/Wow/

Fantastic, sleek, polished and content exploding sites selected for their design, graphic quality, Web resources, coolness or their exploitation (in a good way, of course) of new technology.

Books & Reading

I think it is good that books still exist, but they make me sleepy. – Frank Zappa

Connection

http://www-dept.usm.edu/%7econnect/connec.html

When a project connecting college English majors with eighth grade students was created, this site was born.

This is a place where you can browse quality and acclaimed young adult novels that are perfect for the classroom and read reviews written by young adults. It even includes an opportunity for students to participate in the development of reviews for the website.

Favorite Teenage Agnst Books

http://www.grouchy.com/angstbooks.html

Let's face it, when you're a teenager, your life is angst-ridden — so why shouldn't your books be? Here you'll find the best of teenage angst books, favorite authors such as Judy Blume, in easy-to-view categories. Includes plenty of reviews to let teens know just which books should make it to that summer reading list. Sponsored by Cathy Young.

Historical Fiction

http://falcon.jmu.edu/~ramseyil/historical.htm

The official Internet School Library Media Center's historical fiction page. Not only does this site provide some of the most relevant and engaging books on history, but it also contains links to lesson plans and the best methods of introducing historical fiction to today's stuck-in-the-present students.

Hungry Mind Review

http://www.bookwire.com/hmr/

Not just another list of books for teens. Assembled by some of the best authors, this special list includes books that have a powerful appeal to today's teens and the issues they deal with, as well as personal and often moving comments on how these books influenced the writers who read them. Sponsored by Bookwire.com

Janes Book Page

http://www.geocities.com/Broadway/Stage/4935/

Teens will find great lists of good books here. They can get all the books, reviews, and even recommended reading lists they need to last the entire semester — from biographies and historical works to the latest life-changing fiction.

Recommended Young Adult Reading

http://www.st-charles.lib.il.us/low/ygadread.htm

The best of the best in reading for teens. Includes books taken from the American Library Association's recommended reading lists, these are the books that teens will devour. They are great alternatives to TV, and they include titles for the reluctant reader. This site also offers links to an online bookstore for purchase. Sponsored by St. Charles Public Library.

Booksellers

The book salesman should be honored because he brings to our attention, as a rule, the very books we need most and neglect most. – Frank Crane

Amazon.com

http://www.amazon.com/

The biggest may not always be the best—unless you're Amazon.com. This homepage for world's largest book retailer features millions of book titles—cross-referenced and searchable by author, title and keyword—along with CDs, videos, and z-shops.

Barnes and Noble.com

http://www.bn.com

Their slogan is "If We Don't Have Your Book, Nobody Does" —and BarnesandNoble.com's claim may be true. Their site lists an enormous inventory, author chats, search features, book descriptions, reviews, availability and more.

Bestsellersforless.com

http://www.bestsellersforless.com/

In the face of so much competition, bestsellersforless.com posts its price and service guarantees right in the middle of its homepage. Archives present titles in every major category (both hardcover and paperback), including business bestsellers.

Bookstore Metasearch

http://www.emailman.com/books/metasearch.html

Bookstore MetaSearch powers a potent engine which searches the catalogs of six major online book retailers by author or title. It also links to numerous used and rare book search resources.

Borders.com

http://www.borders.com/

Book resources at Borders include a daily spotlight book, DVD and music title, reviews, bestseller lists, upcoming releases, recommended and bargain selections, book-related news, and extensive inventories of books, DVDs and music.

2MillionBooks

http://www.2millionbooks.com/

2 Million Books & More is a retail site that discounts a combined collection of three million books, movies and music titles. This homepage features bestsellers, featured seasonal titles, and quick access to numerous categorical archives.

Cancer (*See* Health--Diseases and Conditions)

Careers

When you reach for the stars, you may not quite get one, but you won't come up with a handful of mud either. – Leo Burnett

Battle Creek Health Online

http://www.bchealth.com/

This site offers an exciting new way to introduce 11th and 12th grade students to potential career paths in the health care industry. Through this program, students will receive an introduction to health care skills and spend three weeks of each month in a hospital setting for hands-on experience they can't get anywhere else. Better have them try it out, stat. Sponsored by the Battle Creek Health System.

CC: Internship Information

http://www.careermosaic.com/cm/cc/cc3.html

Hands down, one of the best ways to find that practical work experience and on-the-job training that will give students the edge in today's job market. This list of links will take students to some of the top sites that offer complete internship information and programs. Sponsored by CareerMosaic.

Career Choices: Exploring Occupations

http://www.umanitoba.ca/counselling/careers.html

The University of Manitoba offers teens the opportunity to explore different career paths. Links to a variety of sites representing different occupations.

Career Magazine

http://www.careermag.com/

This useful resource contains job postings, search engines, and resume banks to help students find that perfect job. But what makes Career Magazine stand out is their special features that go behind the job postings to help anyone land that perfect job or switch careers. Includes articles, advice columns, job matchings, and motivational pick-me-ups. Career Magazine aids those in search of employment by presenting a selected collection of links to online resources related to career strategies and job opportunities.

Career Resource Center

http://www.careers.org

Career Resource Center is the Internet's most complete and extensive index of career-related websites. It includes over 7,500 links to jobs with major employers (from jobs posted in major newspapers and Internet newsgroups), career tips, and links to colleges, libraries, and employment offices. The links are thorough and exhaustive, and they are also indexed. The site contains a voluminous range of career material, job postings, and sites for the teen job-hunter.

Career Resource Homepage

http://www.rpi.edu/dept/cdc/homepage.html

Voted one of the top 100 sites on the Internet by PC Magazine, and it's not hard to see why. With a massive job database, career placement services, newsgroups, and links to other job sites, this clearinghouse of employment-related information on the Net is nothing short of a career-hunter's best friend. Compiled by Jasmit Singh Kochhar.

Career Toolkit

http://www.myfuture.com/OUTPUT/career.htm

Here you'll find the "resources to do the self-exploration needed to make good career choices, build an excellent resumé, create the right cover letter and get the right mindset for your interview." Many high school grads will attend a four-year college, but over one million teens each year choose something else. This website offers seven different possibilities for the high school graduate.

Careerbuilder

http://www.careerbuilder.com

How do you solve that age-old problem of getting a job that requires experience when you don't yet have it. This site offers several ways to overcome this dilemma for people seeking to get started in new fields—from first-time job seekers to those looking to change career tracks.

CareerCity

http://www.careercity.com

The publisher of the Job Bank books has compiled thousands of links to employers, jobs, and job fairs. For articles on salaries, interviewing, cover letters and follow up, click here.

The Catapult on JobWeb

http://www.jobweb.org/catapult/catapult.htm

A springboard to a career- and job-related information, this site is used by career service professionals from around the world. It includes links to job posting sites, career advice and tips, career library resources, professional development opportunities, and the best in employment publications. Sponsored by the National Association of Colleges and Employers.

Fastest Growing Occupations: 1992–2005

http://www.careermart.com/advise/adbestopps.html

A bare bones page that lists the fastest growing occupations at the turn of the century. Sponsored by Career Mart.

Future Scan

http://www.futurescan.com/

Everyday can be career day with this first interactive career guide for teenagers. It contains strategies for success in the real world, tips on getting your foot in the door, good solid career advice, and more career information and links than you can shake a first paycheck at. If your teens are ready for work experience, but not sure what to expect, the answer is here. It includes links to some of the best career sites, in-depth looks at various careers, and a book full of advice and information to get ready for the first day of work. Sponsored by Tramp Steamer Media, LLC.

Guide to Internet Career Resources

http://www.ukans.edu/~upc/internet.html

The Guide to Internet Career Resources will direct your teens to career information and job listings on the Web, as well as numerous newsgroups, mailing lists and newsletters.

High School Recruiter

http://www.adguide.com/highschool

Adguide's High School Recruiter Employment Site is part of Adguide's family of job sites. This comprehensive job site is for people seeking part-time jobs and full-time career opportunities, and employers who are looking for entry level or experienced employees. Graduates of high schools, technical schools, vocational schools, community colleges, colleges and universities are welcome. Fast, easy and free!

Internet Career Resources

http://phoenix.placement.oakland.edu/career/
Guide.htm

Proclaiming to be the "Definitive Guide to Internet Career Resources", this site provides an extensive alphabetized listing of website links on jobs and careers.

Kaplan Careers

http://www.kaplan.com/

This established educational consultant organization delivers a collection of resources covering issues such as career selection, finding great jobs, preparing resumes and cover letters

Monster.com

http://www.monster.com/

Give students an edge in job hunting with this powerful online career center. Not only will they be able to search for jobs by location and category, but they'll receive advice and tips from behind the scenes experts. Includes a special section for international jobs. Sponsored by Manpower Professional.

Next Step Magazine

http://www.nextstepmagazine.com/

Help students take the step to a great career with this online e-zine. Each month, the magazine features three to five new career profiles of businessmen and women in different professions, as well as tips and advice on life after high school. This will guide students through that overwhelming, yet oh-so-necessary process of getting a job.

Pre-Law.com

http://www.pre-law.com/

This website offers advice on gaining admission to law school for the pre-law student. It features straightforward advice and guidance from professional and experienced pre-law advisors. It offers one full year of unlimited, personalized, high-quality preparation and instruction for one flat fee. Sponsored by the Law School Admissions Council, Inc.

School-to-Careers

http://www.swep.com/schooltocareers/index.html

Changing the way the world learns, School-to-Careers is a new approach to learning that lets students apply what they learn to real-life work situations. This site is packed with useful teacher and student resources, product descriptions, and chapters from online books available for purchase. Sponsored by South-Western Educational Publishing.

Space Careers

http://www.spacelinks.com/SpaceCareers/

Space Careers is a comprehensive one-stop reference source for employment in the space industry. Teens can browse over 500 links directly related to space jobs!

Chat

A friend is a present you give to yourself.
– Robert Louis Stevenson

(Because of the variety of topics that may be discussed in these chat rooms, parents, teachers and librarians may wish to visit these sites before referring teens to them.)

Arrogant Teen Chat

http://www.teenchatroom.com

This site offers different chat rooms geared to different teen interests. Selections include Colleges, Art, Music, Sport, Wrestling, Singles, among other choices. In Teen Chat Rooms #1, #2, #3 or #4, there is always someone to talk to.

Chat-O-Rama!

http://www.solscape.com/chat/

Gargantuan listing of chat groups, and tidbits on how, when and with whom to use them.

Cloud Nine

http://www2.chathouse.com/cloud9/

Chat designed for older teenagers—between the ages of 16 and 19 years old. Meet new people, find keypals, and discuss hot subjects. Teens who use this site, however, need to remember not to give out personal information. Just like in any public setting, you don't really know with whom you are communicating.

Cool Chat

http://www.coolchat.com/

A graphically sharp site offering more than chat rooms. Teens can get their own free Web page, search thousands of "love ads," add their own "love ad," and search profiles to find other teens with similar interests. Choose from over 50 different chat rooms. Sponsored by Cool Chat, Inc.

Getting Real!

http://www.gettingreal.com/

Getting Real helps teens to find someone to talk to who actually understands them—other teens. This powerful and all-together fun chat room will let them talk for hours upon hours with friends from around the corner or around the world. Sponsored by Kidsites 3000, Inc.

OmniChat!

http://www.4-lane.com/index.html

Listing of popular chat sites that cover topics from rock climbing to basketball, hardware to programming, business to religion and politics to music.

the student center

http://s003.infomall.org:8003/cgi-bin/studcent/
cyberpals_high.pl

The Web can be a vast, lonely place, but the cyber student center can help out. Created just for students, this interactive meeting center lets teens hang out and talk about anything and everything through chat rooms and message boards. It gives teens a sense of community through free e-mail and home page services, offering links to the best places to surf. Sponsored by Sports Ent.

Talk City Online

http://www.talkcity.com/

At any given time, this site offers a list of over 100 online conferences or chats, managed by conference hosts.

TeenChat

http://www.chatspot.net/TeenChat/

With chat rooms with names like Flirt Room, The Lounge, Preteen, you can find a chat room about almost anything. Teens can get connected with another teen, read a teen e-zine, participate in a poll on a variety of subjects and post messages on the message board. Sponsored by the ChatSpot Chat Network.

Yahoo's List of Teen Chat Rooms

http://events.yahoo.com/Net_Events/Society_and_Cu
lture/Cultures_and_Groups/Teenagers/Chat_Rooms/

A massive listing of every imaginable type of chat site that pertains to teens. Chat rooms for guys only, for girls only, for young teens, old teens, wannabe teens. You name it, there's a chat room about it. Yahoo sponsored.

College Applications

Those who go to college and never get out are called professors. – George Givot

ASN: Applicant Support Network

http://wl.iglou.com/asn/

Teens can get an insider's view on college admission applications from professionals who have reviewed

actual admission files. This site is full of tips that every student can use to help craft the most effective application possible for graduate and undergraduate schools. Sponsored by Career Advisor Associates.

Accepted.com

http://www.accepted.com/

For students have found the college of their dreams and now only one thing stands in their way— being accepted. Turn the tide in their favor with this professional editing service that assists students with application writing including essays, personal statements, letters of recommendation, and resumes-through their professional staff or free online articles.

Cambridge Essay Service

http://world.std.com/~edit

College and business school application essays made easy! This professional editing staff is ready to unfreeze any student's ideas and demystify the writing process by helping students develop original and personal ideas for the essay, write and rewrite the essay, and prepare an application that stands out from the crowd. A free assessment is available, with fee-based services for more extensive assistance.

CampusBound

http://www.interlog.com/~vacomm/campus.html

Increase a student's chance to get accepted into a top US college and graduate school program with this college applications academy. Services include writing and editing assistance with college application essays, free draft assessments and e-mail consultations, and resources on college searches, application submissions, and financial aid information.

College Choice Website

http://www.gseis.ucla.edu/mm/cc/home.html

This nonprofit information service for college bound students offers everything they need to know about the college selection and admission process. It will help them prepare for college, pick and apply to the right school, provide financial assistance information, and even get them ready for their first year away from home.

College Express

http://www.collegexpress.com/

No strangers to the admissions process, the sponsors of this college advisory site have brought countless students and colleges together for over a decade. Information about particular colleges and universities is offered, as well as advice on colleges in general. Sponsored by Carnegie Communications, Inc.

CollegeApps.com

http://www.collegeapps.com/

This site offers advice to students about applying for college or prep school. It will actually show them how-to-do-it, easily and effectively. The site also promotes their "Show! Don't Tell! How to Personalize College Applications" book (available here for purchase). This book will motivate students, take their fears away, and deliver a sure-fire method of writing essays.

CollegeGate

http://www.collegegate.com/

For a small fee, CollegeGate can take the anxiety out of any student's application process by offering Harvard-trained essayists to help a student prepare an application essay. In addition, they offer free services that will let students research schools online, talk with college counselors and students, and browse their bookstore for great deals on test preparation, essay writing, and college-related books.

Cynthia Good's College and Career Planning

http://users.massed.net/~cgood/

This website offers links, links, and more links to the best college and career planning sites a student could need. It includes sites for finding a college and/or career direction, applying for financial aid, preparing and submitting college applications, prepping for tests, and honing study skills.

ENTA

http://enta.com.au/

For students who are looking to go to college abroad, this is one spot to check. For a fee, this comprehensive service will help students apply to over 1,500 educational institutions world-wide, using a single application form to save them time and money. The system is completely automated and Internet-based. Sponsored by ENTA International.

Embark.com

http://www.embark.com/

A good source for college application forms. Using this site students can submit their application to most major colleges and universities right online—without having to reenter the same information again and again. It's quick, easy, and free (except for the college's processing fee). Sponsored by Snap Technologies.

The Essay Wizard

http://www.northfork.com/essaywiz/

Writing an entrance essay is one of the pre-college student's important tasks. Whether students have no clue where to begin or just need a grammar check, the Essay Wizard will help them with suggestions about style and content and offer lists of resources and tips on the application process for free. For a small fee, the service will personally critique essays on grammar and content.

The Ivy Review

http://www.ivyreview.com/

This offline, private educational consulting group offers classes and tutorial services to any college-bound student. They've already helped scores of students gain admission to the nation's top universities through their strategic academic and financial planning, college and major selection, campus tours, application seminars, and collegiate workshops. Sponsored by the Ivy Review.

XAP Corp.

http://www.xap.com/

This is How-to-Get-into-College 101 for teens. It is an indispensable one-stop source for online college admission applications, financial aid information, career guidance, prep courses, and interactive campus tours. Best of all, it includes an alphabetical and geographical listing to over 3,000 universities and colleges websites. Sponsored by XAP Corporation.

College Entrance Exams

Who dares to teach must never cease to learn.
– John Cotton Dana

ACT

http://www.act.org/

This is the official site of ACT, The American College Testing program. Here, teens can go straight to the source for tips and strategies on testing for college admission, FAQs, and test centers and dates. In addition, students can also find help with college admissions and advising, career and educational planning, student aid, continuing education, and professional certification and licensure.

American College Entrance Directory

http://www.aaced.com/

Relieve the pressure of SATs, ACTs, and college in general with this helpful guide for the students who are seeking to enter college. The site offers tips on registration; application, and submission procedures. Students can also obtain scholarship and financial aid information. Further, there is a list of 3,000 official college and university websites. Sponsored by the American College Entrance Directory.

The College Board

http://www.collegeboard.org/

This is the official online site of the College Board, where they'll guide students in preparing for the SATs and beyond, with college assessment, guidance, admission, placement, financial aid, curriculum, and research. This is an essential resource for students and teachers alike.

College Powerprep

http://www.powerprep.com/

College Powerprep offers a set of comprehensive SAT and ACT preparation tools for purchase, as well as free tips, preparation advice, exam strategies, and resources on college selection, admittance, and financial aid.

College Preparation Services

http://www.college-prep.com/

This site offers fee-based professional assistance to students who are seeking admission to the best American college and universities. The mission of the College Preparation Services is to help students get through SAT and TOEFL testing, and to help them find the right college.

Conquer Math

http://www.conquermath.com/

The mission of this site is to help students improve their SAT math scores with a free online test section that offers instantaneous results and tips. The sponsor also offers an online study guide that can be used at home as a tutorial or in the classroom as a reference. The guide is available in seven different graduate levels.

Princeton Review

http://www.review.com/

One of the nation's most popular standardized test preparation companies now offers students a wealth of free and unique resources right on the Web. Here, students can gather information about tests (from the SATs to the GRE), colleges, admissions, internships, and career programs. Special features include an all-in-one college application tool. Sponsored by Princeton Review Publishing LLC.

SATMath

http://www.satmath.com/

This page offers a set of online math SAT preparation courses which are available for a small monthly fee, as well as free sample preparation materials. Through the website, students can obtain access to diagnostic tests, tutorial sections, simulated SAT tests, and personalized schedules to help them boost their SAT score. Sponsored by Cubic Science Inc.

SSAT: Student Guide Online

http://www.ssat.org/

Students taking the SSATs can get a head start with this online guide that allows them to register for the SSAT online, request test changes and additional score reports, learn about the leading independent secondary schools, and obtain tips on taking the test, as well as sample questions.

testprep.com

http://www.testprep.com/

This SAT prep site offers something that most other SAT prep sites don't—free services. Here, students can use free Internet test preparation software to help them prepare for the SAT and maximize their scores. A more in-depth version is available for purchase. Sponsored by Stanford Testing Systems, Inc.

College Life

Life is like a box of chocolates: You never know what you're gonna get. – Forrest Gump

Bolt College Planner

http://www.bolt.com/

Think of this site as the AOL for college students. It offers instant messaging, chat rooms, horoscopes, entertainment reviews, advice, news, and, oh yeah, that vital information on schools, advice, and the life of a college student.

College Prep 101

http://Collegeprep.okstate.edu

A class any college bound student can't afford to miss. These free real world lessons will help anyone prepare for and select a college, ease the transition, and manage the changes that will occur—written by faculty, staff, and students of Oklahoma State University. Perfect for teachers, too.

CollegeBound Network

http://www.cbnet.com/

A student's interactive guide to college life that's both easy to navigate and as colorful as their own dorm room. Includes the latest noise on college music, all the new developments in technology, an online hangout, cookbook, sports and, of course, college profiles, financial aid, and admission advice.

Collegeways.com

http://www.collegeways.com/

This website is devoted to exploring and discussing the complex issue of student retention and attrition through education-related publications, educational conference presentations, a journal of college student retention, and an enormous list of retention references.

The Quad

http://www.mainquad.com/

Whether its dorm living or the endless bull sessions or the eternal search for a date, the Main Quad replicates student life online. Includes links to financial services, products and entertainment tailored to today's college student.

The Student Survival Guide

http://www.luminet.net/~jackp/survive.html

This site includes: 10 tips for survival in the classroom, 10 tips for improving your writing skills, 10 tips for choosing an effective tutor, 10 things you should know about transcripts, 10 ways to more effectively utilize your time, 10 campus organizations to look into, 10 possible consequences of cheating, 10 things to remember if you're hosting a party, and about 275 more top 10 lists. Sponsored by Jack Pejsa.

The Student Union

http://www.studentunion.com/

The online guide dedicated to life on campus at U.S. colleges and universities takes virtual students on a col-legiate health and fitness tour. Includes links to resources related to student affairs, academic pursuits and social activities.

U., The National College Magazine

http://www.umagazine.com/

Learn about trends and happenings on major college campuses across the United States. Students can register to win scholarships, concert tickets and more online. College trivia, latest campus news, Dear Blabby Contests, polls, and current events. Sponsored by the National College Online Magazine.

College Finance

Why is there so much month left at the end of the money? – John Barrymore

Academic Management Services

http://www.amsweb.com/

Looking for a more convenient and affordable way to pay for education? Students will learn about interest-free monthly payment plans and money-saving loans to help make tuition costs more affordable.

Black Excel: The College Help Network

http://www.blackexcel.org

This college admission and scholarship service helps hundreds of African Americans get into college who might otherwise not have done so. Provides links to scholarship sources, a personalized college help package, a quarterly newsletter, a reference guide to historically black colleges, detailed profiles of individual schools, and a medical school package.

CFI Online

http://www.cfionline.com/

This is a student's guide through the complex and confusing maze known as the "College Financial System." While it is targeted towards financial aid planners, this site can be extremely beneficial for students by giving them a chance to ask the experts about financial aid, as well as teaching them how to conduct their own scholarship search. Sponsored by College Funding and Sparrow & Finch

College Loans and Grants

http://www.fastserve.com/college/

Teens will find that this site offers a complete online guide to financial aid. Through a small monthly fee, students can gain access to everything they need to obtain college financial aid (through several personalized methods) as well as gain access to program information on numerous colleges.

College Parents of America

http://www.collegeparents.org/

This organization is a national membership association dedicated to helping parents prepare and put their children through college. It provides strategies and tips on investing, saving, financial aid, and the many challenges faced by students and parents. It offers newsletters, website updates, and a toll-free hotline. Membership requires yearly fees.

College Planning

http://www.collegeplan.org/

College planning not just for any student, but all students. Whether they are going to school now, planning early, or even going back, students can get the information they need—including college selection, admission, financial aid, and scholarships. Sponsored by Boeing Employees' Credit Union.

The Corporation for National Service

http://www.cns.gov/

This government agency helps students through the red tape by offering payment assistance for college, through service-learning projects in schools. This organization also offers scholarships for young people who serve their communities.

Council for Aid to Education

http://www.cae.org/

A non-profit organization, CAE is dedicated to improving education. Available information includes award programs, assistance in obtaining national and local education support, data on funding, and access to research and contribution publications.

Education Info

http://www.educationinfo.com/

This free source for college and financial aid information is invaluable to any student. Provides a complete list of books and websites designed to help search for college information as well as offer special services and discounts for students. Sponsored by Education Info.

Educational Financial Aid Consulting

http://www.mitchellsweet.com/

One of the nation's leading financial aid servicing and consulting firms offers sound advice for students and their parents who are planning for college.

Kaplan

http://www1.kaplan.com/view/zine/

This site offers additional advice and forms on financing a college education. Cost worksheets, application tips and in-depth information on almost every type of loan imaginable are offered. Sponsored by Kaplan Educational Centers.

Mapping Your Future

http://mapping-your-future.org/

A group of guaranty agencies offer their expertise to students and families about college, career, and financial aid choices. Accurate and up-to-date information can be found on this website. This resource includes online college applications, budget calendars, and a loan calculator. Sponsored by the Texas Guaranteed Student Loan Corporation

My Future

http://www.myfuture.com/

This site offers a compass to any student's future. Fun and interactive, this life guide offers tons of up-to-date facts, figures, and information to help get teens beyond high school. Features include information on financial aid for college, scholarships, getting great jobs (including the military), and managing money.

NASFAA

http://www.nasfaa.org/DoItAffordIt/publicfront.html

Taking the pain out of planning for college, this site is chock full of useful tips and information to get students to take the first step on the right track. Includes information on finding the right college, the right financial aid, and the right tips to a successful college career. Sponsored by the National Association of Student Financial Aid Administrators.

National Alliance for Excellence

http://www.excellence.org/

This non-profit organization, formerly called the Scholarship Foundation of America, is dedicated to providing scholarships to outstanding high school and college students. The site includes information on scholarship programs, how to provide financial and educational support, profiles of award winners, and more.

Sage Scholars

http://www.student-aid.com/index.htm

Worrying about how to pay for college is a big problem for teens and their parents. This college savings program has been designed just for them. While membership is required for a full year before college, this unique investment program could reduce tuition by $13,800 and help make college affordable.

TRAM

http://tram.east.asu.edu/

Funding for college is just a click away with this powerful grant and financial aid search engine. Culled from a vast network of agencies and other top-rated financial sources, TRAM will help any student locate the best research opportunities and funding sources throughout the Internet in a snap.

Tuition Management System

http://www.afford.com/

From payment counseling to help in obtaining federal and private loans, Tuition Management Systems offers innovative monetary services to students and their families so they can truly afford the college of their choice.

U.S. Department of Education Grants

http://gcs.ed.gov/

For teens looking for an education grant, why not refer them directly to the source? This official website of the U.S. Department of Education provides basic, introductory information on how to obtain grants. It includes information on requesting applications, regulations for administering grant programs, as well as the nuts and bolts of grants. Most of the grants described here are for educators, but there are a handful for students.

World of Knowledge

http://www.worldofknowledge.org/

For students who are part of culturally diverse communities, foreign nationals, or immigrants, this non-profit organization may be able to offer assistance on scholarships, grants, and educational materials.

College Search

The terrible thing about the search for truth is that you find it. – Remy de Gourmont

Academic Counseling Services (ACS)

http://www2.interaccess.com/nichenet/acs/

While based in Illinois, this academic counseling service can help students from around the country with their educational and professional life. And with their years of first-hand knowledge of secondary schools, colleges, and specialized institutions, you can be sure they know what they're talking about.

Apply: College Surveys

http://www.WeApply.com/

A student's college savior. From the collegiate experts at Princeton Review, comes this powerful matching service that will take a student's preferences and retrieve a detailed list of the perfect schools for them. Results even include evaluations from the people who know best: the students who go there.

Campus Tours

http://www.campustours.com/

When students can't make it to the campus, bring the campus to the students with these virtual college tours. Just search their extensive database for the desired school to view its static campus shots, interactive maps, college webcams, QuickTime virtual reality tours, and/or online movies.

Campus Visit Travel Desk

http://www.campusvisit.com/

This site tells how to get the most out of a campus visit, and maybe even save a few dollars in the process. While geared towards students interested in Boston colleges and universities, the tips and advice available on this site are a must-see for everyone who's shopping for a college.

College Admissions and Financial Aid Consulting

http://college-solutions.com/

This Kentucky-based offline firm offers students both information and services designed to help them choose a college and gain admission to finding financial assistance. Complete with publications, news, features, and customer testimonials.

College and School Planning Services

http://www.csplan.com/

Does it seem like students have a mountain of college questions? Well, this offline service can provide the answers: advice on what high school curriculum they need, resource material about schools and programs, how to select the perfect school, understanding the application process, preparation for standardized tests, introductions to current students and alumni of colleges, career direction, and interview preparation.

College Foundation Planners

http://www.cfpi.com/

Open the doors to a college education with this complete offline college planning and preparation service. They'll help college-bound students find the best college, get admitted, pay for it without going broke, and actually graduate in four years. Offers test preparation, applications, college and career search, financial aid, and more. Sponsored by College Foundation Planners.

College Guidance Services

http://ultimate.org/2569/

Clarify the confusing college process with this online college guidance service. Offers college and financial aid information, college searches, resume planning, interview prepping, and basic tips for the college beginner—all designed to save students and their families both time and money.

College Visits

http://college-visits.com/

Why settle for a virtual college tour when you can have the real thing led by experienced high school counselors. Offering tours in almost every type of school in almost every region in the U.S., this service will make sure students truly get to know a school. They'll even arrange everything—meetings with admission representatives, student-led campus tours, meals, transportation, and campus housing.

CollegeNET

http://www.collegenet.com/

For students drowning in a sea of college options, here is a site designed to help find the ideal college based on their personal criteria, such as region, major, sports, and tuition. It will even help them find the right scholarship/financial aid and offer the chance to apply online to the college of their dreams. Sponsored by Universal Algorithms Inc.

Counseling and Guidance Links

http://clx.fssc.k12.ar.us/sside/counguid.htm

A great guide for teens and their families. This online resource book will answer almost every question about selecting a college. It includes information on selecting a college, gaining admission, and financing it without going broke. Sponsored by South Side High School.

The Education Network

http://www.ccounsel.com/

Helping with every educational need—from the cradle through college. This site contains over 500 articles, guides, and more, along with professional advice on helping students prepare, find, apply, get to, and survive college. Includes an online store offering CD-ROMs, guides, and college advisors.

Fish Net

http://www.jayi.com/sbi/Open.html

This is the perfect way for students to start thinking about college. This college guide offers a coast-to-coast college search, a form to order college information, expert advice on the college administration process, college applications, and an insider's look at college life. While this site doesn't include every college, the useful information more than makes up for the gaps.

Go College

http://www.gocollege.com/

Everything a student needs to go to college. This collegiate Web source will let your teen find a college, take a virtual tour, locate the right scholarship, apply online, ask the experts a question, and even take a practice SAT or ACT test-absolutely free! It even includes chat rooms and a 24-hour college bookstore.

International Education Service

http://www.ies-ed.com/

Sites on the Internet that helps focus on helping students world wide find and apply to the right school in the U.S. and Canada. By simply completing the International Education Service's application form, foreign students can be matched with the perfect school, college, university, or English language program. And best of all, it's free!

National College Resource Association

http://www.collegeresource.com/

With a few clicks, this site informs students about how to plan ahead for college, choose the best school, choose the right career, apply for grants/scholarship/loans, and even save them money through special discount programs.

PresNet FrontPage

http://pw1.netcom.com/~presnet/index.html

Take all the guesswork out of finding a college with the Presidents' Network. This association will match any student to the right college—even allowing students to apply to 50 colleges with a click of the button. Be forewarned, however, that only schools that partner with them are listed in their database.

Road to College

http://www.roadtocollege.org/

What every student needs to know about college. Based on an hour-long video for West Virginia Public Television, this site offers information on the entire college process, particularly the decisions each student needs to overcome the problems they'll encounter.

Search by Video

http://www.searchbyvideo.com/

Stop the confusing and expensive search for the right college. Without leaving home, students can order for free over 350 college, boarding school, and law school admissions videos to watch right at home—streamlining their search for that perfect school. The tapes even include links to college homepages, directions, and prominent alumni of each college.

Virtual College Day

http://www.criterioninfo.net/vcd/

MSNBC has been hard at work to bring students the easiest way to view college information on the Web. Just pick a multimedia college video through an interactive map or complete college listing and sit back and enjoy the show—there's no more effortless way to find out absolutely everything about a college or university. Requires a video streaming plug-in to view the sites.

Colleges & Universities (*See also* Appendix C: College URLs)

The secret in education lies in respecting the student. – Ralph Waldo Emerson

College and University Home Page

http://www.mit.edu:8001/people/cdemello/univ.html

The perfect start to any student's college search. Pick any of over 3,000 listings to find the official homepage of universities and colleges from around the world—organized alphabetically or by its geographical location. If it's not here, chances are they don't exist—on the Web, anyway.

College Rankings (U.S. News & World Report)

http://www.usnews.com/usnews/edu/college/corank.htm

It's not the size of the school that matters—it's how it's ranked by *U.S. News & World Report*. Here, students can see how the college they're interested in stacks up—ranked by type, region, and even specialty categories such as hottest campus. Includes vital statistics on all schools ranked.

CollegeView

http://www.collegeview.com/

One of the more extensive libraries of college information and multimedia virtual tours on the Web. This free online service provides profiles of over 3,700 colleges and universities, virtual tours of hundreds of schools, electronic applications, financial aid info, career planning tools, chat services, and much more.

Pacific Northwest Colleges and Universities

http://www.wsu.edu:8080/~circlek/pnw/pnw_colleges.html

Teens looking for adventure in the outdoors will find this site useful. It has a complete listing of every college and university located in the great Northwest. Listings include school name, phone number, and website (if applicable) for schools in Alaska, British Columbia, northernmost California, northern Idaho, Oregon, Washington, and the Yukon.

Peterson's

http://www.petersons.com/

One of the most comprehensive college search resources on the Web, sponsored by Peterson's—the world's largest education information and services provider. Here, you can search Peterson's databases that include every private school, college, and university. These resources provide almost everything a student needs to go to college—except the transportation.

Pioneer Planet College Guide

http://www.pioneerplanet.com/archive/colleges/index.htm

A student's best companion to finding the college of their choice on the Web. Organizing the vast resources of the Internet, this site will offer the information they're looking for to make smart decisions—whether through virtual campus tours or detailed information on majors, courses, financial aid, and more.

The Proed Education Inc.

http://webm33f7.ntx.net/proed/

A grand slam of a site for student athletes. PROED specializes in helping any student athlete get into the college of their dreams. They create opportunities by getting students' names out there and recognized, while coaching students on how to choose a school, tell them what to do and when to do it, and showing them the 10-step process to make themselves known to college coaches.

Residential Colleges Worldwide

http://strong.uncg.edu/colleges.html

Listing smaller residential colleges around the world, this site is a perfect resource for those students who want to avoid the "big" schools. Here, students can find that small, faculty-led community of a few hundred individuals.

ScholarStuff.com

http://www.scholarstuff.com/colleges/colleges.htm

Looking for more than just a place to look for schools? ScholarStuff offers students an extensive database of information about colleges and universities around the world. Includes graduate schools, 100,000 sources for financial aid, trivia games, and, for the soon-to-on-your-own student, tons of free stuff.

Universities.com

http://www.universities.com/

Includes an immense database of over 4,500 college and university homepages around the world, a list of credit card companies (to help with the tuition), and numerous calling card sites (to help students call home for money when the credit card runs out).

ULinks.com

http://www.ulinks.com/main.html

If their tremendous index on colleges and universities isn't enough to attract students, then their index of college magazines, financial aid offices, school rankings, and the best school libraries will be. Includes expert advice on college life and beyond.

Y-Life

http://www.zdnet.com/yil/content/college/

Forget about tuition and class size, in today's world it's all about being wired. Here, the technology experts from ZDNET rank colleges by their use of network technology—the way they use technology to support the learning environment.

Computers (*See also* Internet Basics; Website Design)

However far modern science and techniques have fallen short of their inherent possibilities, they have taught mankind at least one lesson: Nothing is impossible. – Lewis Mumford

desktoppublishing.com

http://desktoppublishing.com/

This very well may be the ultimate site for desktop publishing. It boasts over 6,000 pages of information, ideas, products and shareware, so feel free to let your teens explore this site.

Generations: Through the History of Computing

http://www.dg.com//about/html/generations.html

Let your teens take a tour of the history of computing from 1960 through 1996. The tour chronicles the outstanding digital revolution that has taken place in our lifetimes. It all began with transistors and moved onto integrated circuits, microprocessors, and the Intel evolution. Teens can learn about the companies and products that have made significant impact on the evolution of computers. Sponsored by Data General Corporation.

HardwareCentral

http://www.hardwarecentral.com/

A tremendous resource, full of product reviews, articles, discussions, and tips for optimizing and troubleshooting PC hardware. Sponsored by the Internet.com Corp.

SoftGuide

http://www.softguide.com

This is an interactive buyer's guide that helps the student to quickly locate the right software for them. Teens can search using familiar terms, then compare and evaluate products, visit publisher sites, read reviews, download free demos, explore related Web resources, and find the lowest prices.

Computers--Magazines

Whether you think you can or can't, you are usually right. – Henry Ford

Macworld

http://www.macworld.zdnet.com/

For the late breaking news for Mac users, this is a great place to start. This page gives you access to the top stories, plus columns, newsletters, and how-tos. Tabs link to MacCentral, MacWEEK, iMacworld, MacGaming and MacBuy.

PC Guide

http://www.pcguide.com

Teens with technical computer questions will want to visit PC Guide, one of the Internet's premier sites for personal computer reference information. Check the tip of the day, which provides useful and unusual pointers.

PC Magazine

http://www.zdnet.com/pcmag/

ZDNet's PC Magazine Online is at the top of the list for any computer user. It is an impressive, almost overwhelming, site with a lot to offer both teens and adults.

PC World

http://www.pcworld.com/

This magazine offers a first-rate site geared for all levels and ages of computer users. Many will appreciate the

clear style of this site's content. Teen users will be informed, but not intimidated by the news, reviews, and how-to's found here.

Top 100 Computer Magazines

http://www.internetvalley.com/top100mag.html

Computer buffs will appreciate this list of the top one hundred computer magazines from the company that coined the term the term "Web Influence." It is a fascinating site, especially for those looking for some quantifiable means of comparing one magazine to its peers.

Computers--Shareware

Where we all think alike, no one thinks very much. –Walter Lippman

Download.com

http://www.download.com/?st.snap.dir

CNET's Download.com lives up to its name, offering considerable shareware and freeware programs, recommendations and product reviews.

Dr. Download

http://www.drdownload.com/home.htm

This site may not be the largest source of downloadable software, but it emphasizes quality. Tired of wasting time downloading software that doesn't work? Try this site offering only software that has been tested and rated.

Free Yourself Freeware Site

http://www.freewarenet.com/

This website contains an extensive database of high-quality freeware and free software for Windows 95/98, Windows 3.1 and DOS operating systems. Students will also find a comprehensive site directory, a free newsletter, and lots more!

Screen Savers Bonanza

http://www.bonanzas.com/ssavers/

The name of this website pretty much says it all. Teens will find thousands of screen savers in dozens of categories from whimsical to magical, from ugly to religious.

Shareware Junkies for Windows

http://www.sharewarejunkies.com/windows.htm

Shareware Junkies has hundreds of links covering almost every aspect of PC computing. The site is easy for teens to navigate despite its enormity.

Shareware.com

http://www.shareware.com/

Where can you find more than 250,000 different software titles? Shareware.com has shareware in every imaginable category. All are available for immediate download. After selecting the platform, users can conduct a search for any category. The site offers pointers to the latest versions of kid's titles, educational titles, games, etc. Subscribe to their free newsletter delivered to your e-mail address weekly and keep posted on the newest software.

SoftCrawler

http://search.ioc3.de/SoftCrawler/

SoftCrawler is a meta search engine for software. It queries numerous search engines at the same time and displays the results in a sorted list of hits. Instead of having to plow through massive shareware archives, save time by clicking here.

SoftSeek

http://www.softseek.com

SoftSeek, a ZDNet company, is a directory of over 12,000 top-rated shareware titles for Windows. It describes itself as a "source for shareware, freeware, and evaluation software, a huge site that can fulfill every shareware, freeware and evaluation software need." Give it an additional star for a clean, non-distracting interface. Choose from the latest versions of kid's titles, educational titles, games, etc. Teens can subscribe to a free newsletter delivered to their e-mail address weekly that will keep them posted on the newest software.

Topsoft.com

http://topsoft.com

No need to spend a small fortune on software anymore. Teens will love this awesome index of shareware, freeware, commercial software, demos and betas! The extensive archive is updated by software publishers themselves, so it always offers the newest and best.

ZDNet Downloads

http://www.hotfiles.com/index.html

One of the largest listings of free software on the Web! Games, education, kids, graphics, multimedia, and demos are just a few of the available categories, from simple solitaire to awesome action. From starfield simulations to shuttle images to alien invasions, these Space Screen Savers are out of this world.

Computers--Macintosh

Men are only as good as their technical development allows them to be. – George Orwell

Lazerworks

http://www.lazerworks.com/

This site features selected Macintosh games produced since 1998 that are available for purchase in a CD-ROM format. Ordering information and reviews are included.

The Mac Observer

http://www.webintosh.com/

This site offers up a generous mix of Macintosh software previews and reviews, editorial opinions and Mac-related news from many authoritative sources on the Web.

Mac Orchard

http://www.macorchard.com/

Lists over 280 of the best Internet applications for Mac users, with reviews from the Orchard's visitors and links to download sites.

The Mac Zone

http://www.zones.com/

From the Zones.com home page, select MacZone. Teen Mac enthusiasts can locate many consumer-related resources for their Macs at this site, as well as online assistance, software downloads, and items for sale.

MacDirectory

http://www.macdirectory.com/

This definitive Macintosh resource includes over 44,000 products, databases, and services (including consultants, jobs, Macintosh User Groups [MUGs]). Updated daily. Mac enthusiasts will get online assistance, downloads and links to other resources.

Cooking & Food

What this country needs are more homes with good books and less homes with poor cooks. – Anonymous

allrecipes.com

http://www.allrecipes.com/

AllRecipes.com provides a complete menu of featured free recipes and overstuffed categorical archives for baking breads and sweets, soups, and pasta, plus holiday and seasonal items, and a retail link to the Culinary Store.

Copycat Recipes

http://www.copykat.com/

CopyKat Recipes enables teens to cook their favorite restaurant and fast-food dishes, offering thousands of recipes arranged alphabetically by restaurant of origin. Students can learn what's really behind McDonald's "secret sauce" along with recipes from well-known chains like the Olive Garden and Boston Market.

Cyberchef

http://www.cyberchefs.net/

Cyberchef offers "daily specials" with features on seasonal dishes, a culinary tour, renown chef profiles (plus recipes from their kitchens), links to restaurant websites, recipe archives, and more.

Fast Food Finder

http://www.olen.com/food/

Sponsored by Olen Publishing, the Food Finder is a search engine that locates items in nearly twenty major fast food chains by specifying the maximum number of calories, fat, sodium and cholesterol a student's diet allows.

Food-Guide.com

http://www.food-guide.com/

If we are what we eat, then Food-Guide.com can help us know what we are, with recipes categorized by meal and course (including several from M&M, Pillsbury and Ritz) and links to numerous other food-related resources.

Food Stop

http://www.foodstop.com/

Chef Ashbell's Foodstop.com presents American Southern, Creole and Jamaican specialty recipes. A "What's Hot" section includes recipes and tips for a wide range of occasions. It includes reprints, excerpts and recipes from an authentic 1939 southern soul food cookbook—with such colorful names as Kentucky Burgoo and Pot Likker.

Good Cooking

http://www.goodcooking.com/

With a smart and stylish presentation, Good Cooking provides links to culinary institutes and cooking schools, vegetarian and "fat free" resources, fishery and

seafood links, wine and beverage guides, a "suggestion pot," restaurant guide, and plenty of recipes.

Internet Chef

http://www.ichef.com/

The Internet Chef is never too busy in the kitchen to fail to respond to questions. This Internet Chef is a digital magazine that offers recipe archives in dozens of food categories (all keyword searchable), two different chat forums, food "rescue" tips, and more.

joyofbaking.com

http://www.joyofbaking.com

Have a penchant for breakfast pastries, cookies, cakes and tarts? You've come to the right place! Get free RealAudio and Video cooking demonstrations, and recipes for delicious baked goods.

Meals.com

http://www.my-meals.com/

A comprehensive digital combination cookbook/meal planner, Meals.com allows registered members to customize the site and create their personalized recipe box, a weekly meal planning template, and special retail offers. Membership is free.

Mimi's Cyber Kitchen

http://www.cyber-kitchen.com/

A member of the Rec.Food.Cooking Webring, Mimi's CyberKitchen posts free food-themed e-greeting cards, an archive of cookbook reviews, retail links, a recipe archive, exchange board, as well as loads of links to food and culinary supply retailers.

Non-Alcoholic Holiday Recipes

http://www.drmike-hypnosis.com/recipe.html

These non-alcoholic recipes provide liquor-free variations on popular beverage and food recipes that will tickle teen tastebuds, yet keep their eyes clear and focused. Recipes include alcohol-free eggnog, margaritas, white russians, and a New Year's Eve punchbowl.

RecipeCenter.com

http://www.recipecenter.com/

A whopping 100,000 recipes in categorical, keyword searchable archives! The RecipeCenter is a great step to learning how to cook well. It offers a free e-mail daily recipe service, free cooking software, a culinary FAQ, and more. Available in French and German.

Crisis Intervention

I find the great thing in this world is not so much where we stand, as in what direction we are moving.
– Oliver Wendell Holmes

Covenant House

http://www.covenanthouse.org/kid/kid_sui/kid_sui.htm

This is a great resource to help parents and teens alike in dealing with teen suicide issues. Learn the warning signs of teen suicide, understand the reasons and issues suicidal teens struggle with. Get the straight facts, and a toll-free hot line teens can call for help—anonymously and without being judged. Sponsored by the Covenant House.

JagNet Teen Crisis Centre

http://www.geocities.com/TelevisionCity/2427/

For teens dealing with problems with parents, friends, or romance, this online crisis center provides another place to seek advice. Teen to teen advice with services in twelve languages.

Kids-in-Crisis

http://www.geocities.com/Heartland/Bluffs/5400/

The site is strong on information but you won't find snazzy graphics. It does have lots of solid facts about kids in crisis. It provides online support for anyone associated with kids who are experiencing the effects of substance abuse, physical or emotional abuse, mental illness, runaways, sexually transmitted diseases or thoughts of suicide. It describes experiences appropriate for older teens.

PAVNET Online

http://www.pavnet.org/

PAVNET (Partnerships Against Violence Network) Online is a library of information about violence and youth-at-risk, representing data from seven different federal agencies. It is a one-stop, searchable, information resource to help reduce redundancy in information management and provide clear and comprehensive access to information for states and local communities.

Some Things You Should Know about Preventing Teen Suicide

http://www.aap.org/advocacy/childhealthmonth/prevteensuicide.htm

The youth suicide rate has risen dramatically in recent years—enough to make it the third leading cause of death in older teens. Get life-saving facts on teen suicide—including how to quickly spot warning signs and how to successfully prevent it in time. Sponsored by the American Academy of Pediatrics.

Teen Age Grief

http://www.smartlink.net/~tag/index.html

A sensitive and important online service providing grief support to bereaved teens. It describes the possible dangers that face a grieving teen, and it will help parents and educators understand the grief process and unique needs of the teens. In addition, it offers concrete methods to assist the teen in the healing process and get them back into life.

Teen Help

http://www.vpp.com/teenhelp/

More teens than ever before are in need of help, and they, like parents and teachers, can't always do it alone. This website offers shocking reports, eye-opening statistics, and, of course, a toll-free hotline designed to assist parents, teachers, and others in locating appropriate resources for the treatment of struggling adolescents. Sponsored by Viewpoint Productions.

Teen Suicide (APA Online)

http://www.psych.org/public_info/teenag~1.htm

This site explains why and how teens commit suicide with a helpful, life-saving guide to the signs of teenage depression. Included are the latest findings to teen depression and suicide, shocking yet revealing statistics on teen tragedy, and sources where you can find more information and support. Sponsored by the American Psychiatric Association.

Teen Suicide Fact Sheet

http://doncaster.on.ca/~cam/subqueer/pom-fact.html

Did you know that gay and lesbian youth are at least three times more likely than heterosexual youth to attempt suicide? Get the facts on teen suicide, from a different perspective, with this shocking yet all too real teen suicide fact sheet.

The Warning Signs of Teen Suicide

http://www.promina.org/times/issue09a/article09a08.html

Change in eating or sleeping habits, persistent boredom, noticeable personality changes, and cleaning their room can all be signs of teen suicide. Get to know the signals that can mean the difference between life and death from the Promina Health System—including how to take action.

Wizard's Page of Gang-Related Topics

http://www.swcp.com/~cyborg/non-profit/
wizard/index.htm

For years, Phil (the Wizard) Romero, headed one of Santa Fe's largest gangs. Now 28, he spends his time helping troubled youths get out of gangs and stay out of them. His website answers the great questions from kids and parents on gang-related topics and other problems faced by teens.

You Can Handle Them All — Discipline and Behavior

http://www.disciplinehelp.com

This site is not for teens, but could be very useful to those working with them. An exhaustive resource for exhausted parents, teachers and other responsible parties who need additional help to deal with troubled teens. It analytically dissects more than 100 alphabetically arranged behavioral problems into descriptions, effects, corrective actions and related behaviors. Features include a "Behavior of the Day," discussion area, and contact information.

Current Events

There cannot be a crisis next week. My schedule is already full. – Henry Kissinger

CNN Newsroom

http://learning.turner.com/newsroom/index.html

CNN Newsroom is a free online resource designed for teachers but still a valuable website for teens. It features in-depth news stories and world & regional events chosen for their interest to students.
The CNN Student Bureau(CNNSB) is the official newsgathering and reporting program for CNN, offering students the opportunity to be published on the CNNSB website. CNNSB takes the concept of news created for students to the next level by giving students a forum to report the news from their perspective. This site has a section on Electronic Field Trips which includes online tours, teachers resource books, and collections of primary resources, including videos.

Decisions, Decisions Online

http://www.teachtsp2.com/ddonline/

Every month Decisions, Decisions Online showcases a live-action video that presents the clashing viewpoints behind a controversial social issue drawn from today's headlines. Students role-play legislators faced with a

critical situation, Decisions, Decisions Online will stimulate discussions that start inside the classroom and will continue outside of it. Topics include Juvenile Crime, Free Trade, Animal Testing, Death Penalty, Cloning and Gun Control. Sponsored by educational software leader, Tom Snyder Productions.

Hot News/Hot Research

http://poynter.org/dj/shedden/index.htm

The Hot News/Hot Research website is a collection of online resources on current and previous news topics, with an emphasis on stories that have been in the news over several week and written about in multiple sources. Topics go back to 1995 and include stories such as the sarin nerve gas attack in Japan, the 1996 Presidential election, the Unabomber trial, and the Winter Olympics. About once a week the site posts one new topic. URLs are continually updated so the information at the site is current. Sponsored by the Poynter Institute, a school for journalists, future journalists, and teachers of journalism.

Magellan Internet Guide

http://198.3.103.214/education/reference/news_
and_magazines/current_events/

In addition to being a search engine for the entire World Wide Web, this site specializes in news sites that double as ideal resources for the study of current events. All of the major news gatherers from ABC News to the *New York Times* to MSNBC provides students immediate access from this convenient launch pad. Catch the Web version of the venerated television news broadcast, PBS:Online News Hour. Live@ allows students to watch any live event on the Web, from press conferences to sports.

News Directory

http://www.newsdirectory.com/

News Directory is a no frills listing of worldwide magazines, newspapers, television stations. It boasts over 17,000 links to both regional and international news sources. Just click on a continent and then a country and dozens of listings for the magazines and newspapers of that area are easily accessible. You can search by the publication name or the geographic location.

The Paperboy: Online Newspapers

http://www.thepaperboy.com/

With access to links for over 2000 newspapers throughout the world, this is an impressive research tool. Students who are doing reports on current events can obtain a variety of national and world perspectives and impressive quotations. For surfers who want online versions of the *Times*, be it New York, Los Angeles or London, this is the place to look.

Policy.com

http://Policy.com/

Presenting news and analysis about U.S. policies and their international implications, the Policy.com website offers a Washington news java ticker, daily news briefs, a more extensive examination of the "Issue of the Week," and similar features.

TIME for Kids

http://www.timeforkids.com/TFK/

Sponsored by *Time Magazine*, this is the pint-size and online version of the popular news magazine. Also available in a newstand edition and in Spanish. Departments include the Top Story, Election Connection, Kid's Views on the News, World Report, News Scoop, Heroes for the Planet and sections for Teachers and Parents.

Virtual NewspaperCollection

http://www.edoc.com/jrl-bin/wilma/nws

Students can check out this virtual newsstand to get links to more than 100 online newspapers from around the world. It provides quick and easy access to daily and weekly digital publications.

World News for Children (*Tomorrow's Morning*)

http://www.morning.com/currentissue/currentissue
.html#global

This online version of the *Tomorrow's Morning* bi-weekly newsmagazine for children posts highlights from the national, international, political, science and nature, sports, entertainment, and editorial sections of the print edition. It also provides access to archived back issues, subscription information (both for individuals and classrooms), and online brain-teasing contests.

Dance

Life is like music; it must be composed by ear, feeling, and instinct, not by rule. –Samuel Butler

Artslynx International Dance Resources

http://www.artslynx.org/dance/

An impressive list of dance websites that covers employment resources, dance-related artwork international dance competitions, dancer health and safety resources, ethnic dance resources, dance funding and listserv and usenet groups for connecting to dancers throughout the world. Sponsored by Artslynx, an organization dedicated to promoting dance. Some original material published here in addition to extensive collection of websites.

Sapphire Swan Dance Directory

http://www.SapphireSwan.com/dance/

Whether its Balkan dance all the way through the alphabet to the Zydecon style of dance, you will find a thorough and comprehensive database of dance listings at this directory. Some unique categories not found in the other sites listed here include Belly Dancing, Flamenco Dancing and Vintage Dance. This listing will point anyone looking for dance links in the right direction. Some graphics and photographs would dramatically enhance the aesthetic appeal of the site, but what it lacks in style, it makes up in content.

World Wide Web Virtual Library Dance

http://www.artswire.org/Artswire/www/dance/
dance.html

This is a comprehensive directory of information pointers to dance-related sites available on the World Wide Web. For students looking for a listing of dance schools, this site includes both college and university programs. It also features an alphabetical listing of every type of dance from Ballet to Latino to Western Square Dancing. Excellent for searching for funding sources, newsgroups, mailing lists, publications, advocacy resources, competitions, calendar listings, and other dance directories. It is co-sponsored by Arts Wire and DanceUSA.

Dictionaries & Thesauri

The unhappiest of mortals is the writer of dictionaries. Every other author may aspire to praise. The lexicographer can only hope to escape reproach. – Samuel Johnson

Dictionary.com

http://dictionary.com/

This is not only a dictionary, but a place where students can go for help with grammar, usage, style guides and references, and definitions of computer terms and other technical talk. And, it is very user friendly. Sponsored by Lexico LLC.

One Look Dictionaries

http://www.onelook.com/

Stuffing every dictionary on the Internet into one teeny little search engine, this dictionary haven will find the perfect word and definition. All students have to do is type the word they're looking for once to see multiple listings and definitions—ensuring that they find the word, spelling, and definition that they need, every time. Sponsored by Arvic Search Services Inc.

The Semantic Rhyming Dictionary

http://www.link.cs.cmu.edu/dougb/rhyme-doc.html

Few sites are this straightforward. Enter a word, click, and a list of words that rhyme is returned. Teens may be surprised by the number of words they'll get, but easy options exist for narrowing the search scope.

Thesaurus.com

http://www.thesaurus.com/

Anyone doing serious writing or anyone wanting to improve their vocabulary should bookmark this site. It is easier than the print version. Sponsored by Lexico LLC.

tralang's Translating Dictionaries

http://dictionaries.travlang.com/

This site offers free access to online translating dictionaries. Most combinations of the major Western European languages are covered.

Word Focus

http://www.wordfocus.com/

Students of words will find their "Words' worth" at this resource, which includes extensive lists of oxymora, pleonasms, definition activities and more. Membership is required for access to certain site functions (like the advanced search), but it costs nothing except the time to register. The site also links to language arts products at a retail site.

The Word Page

http://users.aol.com/jomnet/words.html

The Word Page posts ten new words each week in a hyperlinked matrix that automatically displays the classification, root(s), similar words, additional explanation and a sentence example of proper use. The ten vocabulary examples and annotations from the previous week are also available.

Wordsmyth

http://www.wordsmyth.net/

Researchers and students can use this website to find definitions, proper pronunciation, parts of speech, and related words (synonyms, antonyms, derivatives, variant forms and cross-references) for almost any English language word. Other features include a "Wordlink" contest, the "Question of the Month" and "Words of the Week," links to other dictionary and thesaurus resources, and a spotlighted ESL site.

Distance Learning

Without education, you are not going anywhere in this world. – Malcolm X

Cyberschool

http://CyberSchool.4j.lane.edu/

Sponsored by the Oregon Public Education Network, this cyberschool offers everything for conducting high school classes in its online curriculum. Separate links provide an explanation of cyberschool, its background and accreditation, course listing and costs, online registration, and affiliated programs. Also link to sponsors of and grants awarded to this project.

Distance Education Clearinghouse

http://www.uwex.edu/disted/home.html

An extension of the University of Wisconsin, this clearinghouse for distance education provides an abundance of links to cyber-education resources. Begin with the Glossary, Definitions, and Introduction. Keeping Current posts timely news and articles (including items about funding and legislation). Also offers links to education technology sites, as well as the University's own distance education curriculum.

TEAMS Distance Learning

http://teams.lacoe.edu/

Tour the virtual classrooms and programs housed by the largest interactive distance learning provider in the U.S. Visit each academic department, survey online libraries and reference sources, and review lesson plans by subject and grade. A service of the Los Angeles Dept. of Education for students from kindergarten through grade twelve.

Drama (*See* Theatre)

Drugs (*See* Substance Abuse)

Drivers Education

Travel is ninety percent anticipation and ten percent recollection. – Edward Streeter

Drivers.com

http://www.drivers.com/

Before teenss hit the road (or anything on it), have them take a test drive at this site devoted to everything on driving. A terrific resource for automobile safety, training, and education as well as the latest news and innovations on the driving scene. Sponsored by PDE Publications.

GA: Driving Tips for Teens

http://www.genacc-us.com/teentips.htm

Before you gas up for Driver's Ed, make a pit stop here for some helpful driving tips. Fill up on surprising statistics and suggestions that will help prevent accidents for new and inexperienced drivers. Sponsored by General Accident Insurance.

Teen New Drivers' Homepage

http://www.teendriving.com

More helpful than a passenger side airbag, these safe and practical tips for new drivers will make any Driver's Ed class, and local roads, run smoother and safer. Includes tips such as driving around town, driving in bad weather, and the all worrisome "should I pass or not?"

E-Mail

Two monologues do not make a dialogue. – Jeff Daly

Angelfire

http://email.angelfire.com/

Totally free e-mail accessible from any computer in the world via the Web. Powered by Who Where?

Beginners' Guide to E-mail

http://www.webfoot.com/advice/email.top.html?
  Yahoo

Brief introduction to the concept and process of sending and receiving electronic mail. Includes page layout and jargon.

Happy Puppy

http://mail.happypuppy.com/aboutus/oneofusa.htm

Web-based e-mail account includes address books, spell checking, and the ability to manage other e-mail accounts directly from user's own browser.

Hotmail

http://www.hotmail.com/

Register as a user for free with this e-mail service provider. Access all the facilities of normal e-mail over the Internet.

Juno

http://www.juno.com/

Advertiser-sponsored free Internet e-mail service for U.S.-based Windows users—no monthly, hourly, membership or other fees.

Lycos E-mail

http://email.lycos.com/member/login.page

This name-powered service allows users to read e-mail on the Web, forward messages anywhere, or read e-mail through a favorite e-mail program.

E-Zines & Magazines

Nothing is so simple that it cannot be misunderstood. – Jr. Teague

Blast Online

http://www.blastmag.com/

This teen magazine features interviews, articles, columns, news items, fashion tips, and everything you might expect from a slick, glossy newsstand magazine, but exceedingly better organized and written. The surprising part? It's done by high school kids from across the country. Sponsored by Day Communications, Inc.

CKOL CityKids Online

http://www.citykids.com

The CityKids Foundation teaches young people problem-solving and decision-making processes that include themselves as part of the solution. Through programs focusing on self-esteem, health and education, CityKids learn to communicate positive values to their peers. CityKids' powerful messages are shared via grass roots programs, television appearances, live CityKids, Repertory performances, videotapes, books, interactive workshops, events,focus groups, and other innovative youth communications. CityKids' programming is open to all youth willing to respect the CityKids principles and demonstrate a commitment to themselves.

DailyStory

http://www.dailystory.org/

While school may prepare your teenage students for life as an adult, who's going to get them through life now? DailyStory is a site for teens from teens. Here, teens can express and learn to deal with their feelings, concerns, fears, and any struggle they may.

Duff

http://www.duff.net/tx/duff/

A colorful, well laid out site that lets teens go directly to the heart of the matter: fashion, chat rooms, columns, opinions, activities, and fun. Furthermore, it doesn't forget that being a teen isn't only about heartbreak and angst, it's about fun and laughter.

E-Zine List

http://www.meer.net/~johnl/e-zine-list/

Young people seeking a comprehensive resource on e-zines will appreciate this list of electronic magazines from around the world. All the listed titles are accessible via the Web, FTP, and/or e-mail. It is updated approximately monthly, and currently contains almost 4000 entries.

First Cut

http://www.firstcut.com/

A slick and stylish news magazine that may look fluffy, but it hides real bite underneath. Based on the award-winning weekly teen magazine show from San Francisco, this website version perfectly channels all that matters to teens—groundbreaking news, music profiles, latest technology, and fashion stories—presented in a format that really gets them to think. Sponsored by KRON-TV and SF Gate.

The Flying Inkpot's Zine Scene

http://inkpot.com/zines/computer.html

Teens seeking further information on zines will be delighted with this site, which offers a substantial list of links to online magazines of all types.

GRIP Magazine

http://www.gripvision.com/

This free online e-zine includes a scholarship and financial aid database, campus programs, a list of the most

useful Internet links, news, views and reviews, and even an extensive opinion forum. Sponsored by GRIP Publications, Inc.

Generation in Circuit

http://www.community.net/~gic/

A teen's e-mail is the equivalent of forming his or her own community. Let them make their voices heard! To these ends, GiC produces a zine available via the web, written for, by and about young people.

The InSite

http://www.talkcity.com/theinsite/index.html

InSite is a place for teens to turn their world around. Teens can find the information, inspiration, and a helping hand to guide them through growing up— from relationships and self-image to getting their own place.

JUMP Online

http://www.jumponline.com/

Ever wonder what happens in the day in the life of a runaway? Which vitamin can help someone remember all those history facts for that world history test? It's all here and plenty more. Get a Makeover, 16 Reasons to Go Solo, Random Spam Question, Are you a Cloner or a Loner?

Living with Parents

http://www.fcs.wa.gov.au/lwp/

A well-thought-out, caring, and easy-to-read guide to one of teenagers' greatest challenges: living with their parents. Looking at both sides of the issue, this site offers insight on how teens and parents think while trying to bridge the gap with ways to communicate, build trust, cope, and plan some fun family activities. It just may surprise you. Sponsored by Family and Children's Services.

National Geographic Society: WORLD Magazine

http://www.nationalgeographic.com/world

This electronic version is much spunkier than the print magazine ever was. It contains great graphics, an easy-to-read layout and many interesting features. Users can search the huge library, check out the mini online encyclopedia, get a complete geography education with the GeoChallenge and Xpeditions, and see the World Geographic Magazine for Kids. Sponsored by the National Geographic Society.

NewsDirectory

http://www.newsdirectory.com

This is an excellent resource for online magazines and newspapers maintained by a print media publication. Students navigating the logically organized index will discover it is extremely easy to use, and the content selection is outstanding.

Nomad, The Brat Journal

http://www.nomad-tbj.com/index.html

United States military brats are people too. That's what this international magazine wants to say to the world, anyway. Catering to the needs of the children of military personnel everywhere, this website offers online profiles of life at military bases across the world, as well as an opportunity to subscribe to the print magazine.

Oblivion

http://www.oblivion.net/

This e-zine focuses on youth, youth issues, and things that are just a bit out of whack. Students can find everything, from news briefs and columns to stories and artwork—with a few links to other teen sites for good measure.

React.com

http://www.react.com/

This is a stylish and colorful online teen magazine that offers a little bit of everything that matters to teens. A weekly poll, joke of the day, place to voice their opinion, view and debate the latest issues, play games, participate in surveys and sweepstakes. Get and give advice, and learn about ways to make a difference. Sponsored by ParadeNet Inc.

Techno Teen

http://www.technoteen.com/

The website made for teens by teens—100%. Not only is this a great demonstration of what teens can do when they set their mind to it, but a great place for teens to hang out. Includes a chat, student e-mail directory, penpal section, and a way to poll other students.

Teen Exchange

http://teenexchange.miningco.com/

A guide to the Internet for young adults. Here, teens can get advice, read the articles on the latest trends, chat, send free e-cards, and, best of all, link to the best sites on the Web dealing with everything they care about—from college information and comedy sites to

online games and teen zines. Sponsored by General Internet, Inc.

Teen Online

http://multihome.www.opus1.com/emol/teenonline/

Although a bit bare in the style department, this site still provides plenty of value with its articles, advice, news, and links to everything teen. Created by students enrolled in a journalism training program and sponsored by EMOL.org—the Entertainment Magazine On-Line.

Teen.com

http://www.teen.com

A multi-layered site with gobs of things to do and places to go for every teen. A Daily Rag, a diary, horoscopes, advice, quotes, riddles, poetry, pearls of wisdom, news headlines, newsletters, soap operas, spiritual center, trivia, weird news, word of the day, contest, polls, free e-cards, free stuff, homework helper, games, shopping, are just a few of the sections teens can surf to within this site. Gotta a few months to kill?

TeenGrrl

http://www.teengrrl.com/

This site is intended for teenage girls with "a thirst for the extreme and a hunger for the alternative." Translation: it has the coolest online chats and articles on everything that's important to a teenage girl— music, clothes, romance, and yes, even school. Sponsored by Last Resort Designs.

Teens Only!

http://education.indiana.edu/cas/adol/teen.html

This is the end-all, be-all of electronic resources just for teens. It offers teens the coolest online teen magazines, TV/radio/movie schedules, teen organizations that make a difference, books and information to help them survive school and the real world, and, of course, the coolest places on the Web to hang out and directions to where the fun is. Sponsored by the Center for Adolescent Studies at Indiana University.

TeenVoice.com

http://www.teenvoice.com

Hackensack University Medical Center sponsors this site that features teen fashion, sports, news, education, careers, faith and values, health and other issues relating to teens. It also includes links to book stores, music stores and classified ads.

Tiger Beat

http://www.tigerbeat.com/

The online version of the popular teen newsstand magazine is filled with quizzes, pin-ups, interviews, and teens' favorite celebrities. While not as inclusive or stylish as the newsstand magazine itself, it still packs the same punch. Sponsored by *Tiger Beat Magazine* and Sterling/MacFadden Partnership.

Word

http://www.word.com/index.html

This sophisticated e-zine offers an innovative look at popular culture. Unique images, graphic designs, typestyles and articles, ideal for the older teen. Every day there is a featured article which is either a parody or satire or spoof. Worth checking out just to see how far to the edge a site can go.

YO!

http://www.pacificnews.org/yo/

YO! connects young people with each other and gives adults a window into the constantly changing cultures of youth. Sponsored by Pacific News Service (PNS), an international network of writers, scholars and journalists.

You!

http://www.youmagazine.com/

Catholic school teachers and students looking for a fun and entertaining site that builds up moral and spiritual values will enjoy this online magazine. An international, multi-award winning Catholic youth magazine, it features entertaining interviews, news, reviews, games, and features — all with a religious spin. Sponsored by Veritas Communications, Inc.

Youth@Valleylinks

http://www.valleylinks.net/youth@valleylinks/

What began as a small local teen e-zine, this website has expanded as it unites teens from across the world. Every teen will relate to, and relish, the fashion/music/game reviews, Dr. Smooth's advice for the lovelorn, and the skinny on wuz happenin' in the teen world today. Sponsored by ValleyLinks and Irenyx Data Group Inc.

Eating Disorders (*See* Health--Diseases and Conditions)

Economics (*See* Finances)

Employment (*See also* Careers)

From what we get, we can make a living; what we give, however, makes a life. – Arthur Ashe

Career Advising and Planning Services (CAPS)

http://muse.widener.edu/CAPS/Resources.html

Hone students' self-assessment, decision-making, and job search skills with this ultimate career development site. It includes help with resumes and cover letters, interviewing, career choices, internships, summer jobs, and, of course, that job of their dreams. Sponsored by Widener University.

Catapult on JobWeb

http://www.jobweb.org/catapult/catapult.htm

A well-organized, indexed listing of websites for job seekers and recruiters.

Cool Works

http://www.coolworks.com/

This site offers links to more than 75,000 really interesting jobs in some great places, like dude ranches and ski resorts. It offers information on opportunities for both seasonal and permanent jobs.

Employment Projections

http://stats.bls.gov/emphome.htm

For those teens who are really serious about career trends, this site offers information about the U.S. labor market for ten years in the future, including labor force trends by sex, race, and age, plus employment trends and their implications.

Internship Resources on the World Wide Web

http://www.cc.colorado.edu/careercenter/summerjobsandinternships/intern.html

Stop hitting the pavement for those internships and hit the Web instead. This is the ultimate list of internship sites and information on the Internet. With just a click of the mouse, anyone can find a perfect internship in computers, health, public service, communications, or any field in which they're interested. Sponsored by Colorado College.

Int'l Study and Travel Center

http://www.istc.umn.edu/

This is the place for those teens with aspirations of studying, working, or traveling abroad. Sponsored by the University of Minnesota, it also features detailed information about opportunities in a different country each week.

JobFactory.com

http://www.jobfactory.com/

This resource can be your best friend in finding a new job. It permits the user to search hundreds of thousands of job openings across the country, link to thousands of sites that post job openings, call thousands of telephone numbers that provide recorded employment information, visit top career sites to best prepare you for the interview and job, link to hundreds of major newspapers' classified sections, or meet with hundreds of top recruiters. Sponsored by the Job Factory.

JobProfiles.com

http://www.jobprofiles.com/

Get the inside scoop on job requirements for differing industries ranging from agriculture, arts, and government, to retail and transportation from people who are actually working in these jobs.

100 Hot Jobs & Careers

http://www.web21.com/jobs/

As the title promises, this is a list of the 100 most popular websites on jobs and careers, many of special interest to teens.

Quintessential Career

http://www.quintcareers.com/

This site offers a comprehensive package of information and resources about jobs and careers. The site's primary focus is on helping college students find internships and employment. In addition to an impressive list of networking strategies, resume writing tips, and other typical job hunter's resources, teens will find a salary negotiation tutorial, an interviewing tutorial, a guide to researching companies, and resources about volunteering. Sponsored by Stetson University.

SummerJobs.com

http://www.summerjobs.com/

This is the perfect site for students seeking some job experience or just a little extra spending cash for the summer. It includes thousands of jobs listed by name and location, job postings for employers, summer jobs, success stories, and tons of links to other great employment sites. Sponsored by Fishnet NewMedia. Search is by keyword or location through this database of worldwide, seasonal, and part-time job opportunities.

Encyclopedias

Nobody gets to live life backward. Look ahead, that is where your future lies. – Ann Landers

Britannica Online

http://www.britannica.com

The Encyclopedia Britannica is home to over 12,000 images, 72,000 articles, and it's now available free of charge. However, the website has proven so popular that you might have to wait to gain access.

Encyberpedia

http://www.encyberpedia.com/

A treasure chest of information and retail services, this site offers a searchable encyclopedia, indexed into nearly one hundred topical categories, and more: Included are links to news from the U.S. Senate, sports updates, a weather tracker; and retail links to purchase a variety of different products ranging from vacuum cleaners and antiques, to stocks and bonds, and travel packages. Site by Voltage.com.

Encyclopedia of Women's History

http://www.teleport.com/~megaines/women.html

Written by and for students from kindergarten through twelfth grade, this searchable encyclopedia presents biographical information about the women who helped shape American and world history. Students can learn about everyone from Abigail Adams, one of the first promoters of women's rights, to skating champion Kristi Yamaguchi, and just about every famous woman in between. The biographies are arranged in alphabetical order.

Encyclopedia Smithsonian

http://www.si.edu/resource/faq/start.htm

The Smithsonian has an excellent database where teens can search through topics such as anthropology, astronomy, archaeology, American social and cultural history, and that's just some of the A's. It also features a Frequently Asked Question section that covers a great number of public inquiries covering a wide range of topics.

Encyclopedia.com

http://encyclopedia.com

Encyclopedia.com is a great solution for teens who need a quick and easy way to start their research quickly and easily.It places an extraordinary amount of information about the world at their fingertips. Site by Infonautics Corp.

Funk & Wagnalls Knowledge Center

http://www.funkandwagnalls.com/

Join (for free!) and get the complete Funk & Wagnalls online encyclopedia, enriched with animations, sounds, music, flags, maps and more, updated monthly. It also includes the Random House Webster's College Dictionary; and Reuters World News Service with the latest updated headlines.

Internet Encyclopedia

http://clever.net/cam/encyclopedia.html

This is an encyclopedia of Internet information divided into two categories. The Macro Reference contains references to large areas of knowledge, FAQs where available, and links to relevant areas. The Micro Reference contains brief bits of information on a multitude of topics.

letsfindout.com

http://www.letsfindout.com/

This is great homework helper where teens can access information on a variety of subjects, or browse links to other cool sites.

Fashion & Beauty

Beauty is in the heart of the beholder. – Al Bernstein

Angel of Fashion

http://www.fashionangel.com/angel.html

Students will find links to everything that's in fashion. It includes information on the pioneering fashion companies, online clothing stores, award-winning designers, models, cosmetics, alternative fashion, fashion zines, and every possible site that's devoted to making people look good. Sponsored by Fashionangel.com

Elle Magazine

http://www.ellemag.com/

Elle Magazine is more than just a pretty face, or a website, for that matter. It is chock full of fashion, tips, guides, models, special features (like interactive makeovers), and their monthly magazine's articles. Elle will always keep teen girls in fashion. Sponsored by Hachette Filipacchi Magazines.

Fashion and Beauty Internet Association

http://www.fbia.com

This site features a unique collection of businesses and individuals who are, or want to be, involved in fashion and beauty on the Internet. Students will reap the benefits by gaining instant access to fashion features, articles, and reviews from the best fashion sites around the world. Sponsored by the Fashion Beauty Internet Association.

Fashion Icon

http://www.fashion-icon.com

For young women who want to be in style, this site brings teens the latest in fashion news, gathering information from every single facet that the Hope diamond of fashion has to offer. From street style to design room fittings and backstage at the shows, there is no fashion detail too small to escape this fashionable site. Sponsored by Fashion Icon.

Fashion Net

http://www.fashion.net

The place to be in fashion — whether it's to get the latest style, news, gossip, or shopping sites. With chat rooms, message boards, and links to all of the Net's most stylish shopping sites (including The Gap, Revlon, and Donna Karan), Fashion Net is a teen's one stop fashion shopping guide. Sponsored by Triple International.

Fashion Planet

http://www.fashion-planet.com

This is one of trendiest sites about fashion — and it's got the awards to prove it. This fashion e-zine includes daily updated news (covering collections, trends, activities, and personalities), true stories and fascinating gossip, tips, and a real online shopping center to tame that fashion beast.

Fashion Showroom

http://www.fashionshowroom.com/

Click onto this collage from the latest collections of prominent fashion designers. It features a gallery of runway fashion photographs and fashion collection photographs.

Fashion Trip.com

http://www.fashiontrip.com/

Before your teens step into that shop, better have them consult their personal online fashion consultant or browse their online e-zine for the latest in styles, news, views, and tips galore. If they're feeling a little out-of-fashion, have them enter a 3D store and see the latest styles, mix and match outfits while they chat, and get personalized fashion and beauty tips from the experts. Sponsored by ModaCad, Inc.

Gladrags

http://www.internetindia.com/GLADRAGS/

India's largest and most reputed modeling agency comes to the Internet in style. Structured to display and find models, this site also offers fashion tips, a rare look at India's entertainment celebs, and articles that deal with issues of concern. Sponsored by Pure Tech India Ltd.

Hair Boutique

http://www.hairboutique.com/

The Hair Boutique is out to banish bad hair days forever. Girls can get tips, articles and product reviews, in addition to visiting the All About Hair and the Salon Web, and shop the marketplace for decorative hair ornaments.

Fashion Carrer Center.com

http://www.fashioncareercenter.com/

For teens interested in a career in fashion, refer them to this employment classified site for the fashion world. Here, anyone interested in making it into the fashion world can post their resume and qualifications for thousand of companies and recruiting firms to see around the world. A great stepping stone to a prosperous fashion career.

Lumiere Magazine

http://www.lumiere.com

Now, your teens can stay one catwalk-step ahead of fashion with this ultimate fashion e-zine. Includes the latest fashion news, outfits, models, makeup tips, and absolutely everything that has to do with fashion —

from the people in the know. Sponsored by Triple International Ltd.

Total Fashion Page

http://www.magna.com.au/~slade/fashion.html

This is students' link to fashion down under. The Australian-based site will link them to the best sites in fashion—designers, history, modeling agencies, shopping malls, education, cosmetics, and museums. And if they can't find what they're looking for, try this site's powerful search engine. Sponsored by Michelle Slade.

Finances

Money is better than poverty, if only for financial reasons. – Woody Allen

Consumer Education for Teens

http://www.wa.gov/ago/youth/

Everything a teen needs to know to avoid getting ripped off can be found at this site. Created by the Washington State Attorney General's Office, this informative and fascinating site gives teens insight on how to become educated consumers through tips and facts on credit cards, telemarketers, music clubs, car buying, and more.

EduStock

http://tqd.advanced.org/3088/

Buy! Sell! Learn? Teens get to know the stock market from the ground up with this instructional site that will teach anyone about the stock market and how it can work for them. It includes tutorials, company information, a real-time simulation, and research tips.

Independent Means

http://www.anincomeofherown.com/

Give female teens a head start in the rat race with this leading provider of products and services for girls' financial independence. This site is the first stop for news on starting a business; making, saving, growing, and utilizing money; and, best of all, networking with mentors who've been through it all.

Investing for Kids

http://tqd.advanced.org/3096/

Bubble gum up three-eighths? Here, teens can learn about stocks, bonds, mutual funds, and any other type of investing. While this site is geared towards younger teens, all ages can benefit from the principles of saving and investing in terms everyone can understand. And, if they're feeling daring, teens can try their own hand at a stock game. Site by Think Quest.

Personal Finance 101

http://www.ralphphillips.com/personalfinance/

Looking to prepare students for some financial security? Then shed a little light on the complexities of personal finance with this insightful guide to everything about finance—from credit cards and saving accounts to life insurance and mutual funds. It's all here to help anyone plan wisely for the future.

Young Investors Web Site

http://www.younginvestor.com/pick.shtml

This guided tour to investing begins with the selection of a nickname, a style button, then choose a tour guide to begin your adventure. This educational site is dedicated to teach young people about investing and finances. Sponsored by Liberty Financial.

For Girls

Femininity appears to be one of those pivotal qualities that is so important no one can define it.
– *Caroline Bird*

Girl Tech

http://www.girltech.com/

This is a fantastic site devoted to girls with an adventurous spirit. It offers lots of well done articles and features all pertaining to empowering women to become the very best they can become. There are biographies of infamous and famous women in the "Her Story" section, including female inventors who changed the world. There are resources for young inventors, and Game Café has lots of fun games to play on or offline with or without friends. Sponsored by Radica Games, Inc.

Daughters of the Moon/ Sisters of the Sun

http://www.daughters-sisters.org/

The Daughters/Sisters Project provides focus groups for young women and men, GenderTalks, workshops and programs. Their mission is to empower young women by fostering mentoring relationships. The project creates ways to bridge the gender, culture, and generation gaps. When girls and young women share their experiences with each other, their self esteem and self worth strengthen.

Girl Power!

http://www.health.org/gpower/

A national public education campaign, Girl Power! encourages 9- to 14-year old girls to make the most of their lives by targeting health messages to girls unique needs and interests.

Girl Zone

http://www.girlzone.com/

This is an online magazine that emphasizes that there is more to being a girl than just looks. This powerful and influential publication is the perfect resource to encourage girls to find their strengths, use their voices, and fulfill their dreams. It is a well-organized, attractive site that covers everything—from sports and music to careers and self-esteem.

Gold Key Circle

http://www.agirlsworld.com/clubgirl/gold-key/index.html

Girls can obtain free membership in this private chat club if they write an article that is published on the site or if they win one of the monthly contests. The chat area features a real-time, passcode-secured chat area just for club members. Girls can participate in special online events with chat guests or serve as hosts in ten chatrooms. It offers great games, quizzes, and prizes for sleepovers, and cool graphic collectibles such as bumper stickers and buttons for girls to print.

Guerrilla Girls

http://www.guerrillagirls.com/

The Guerrilla Girls are a group of women artists and arts professionals who make posters about discrimination. Here is what they say about themselves: "Dubbing ourselves the conscience of the art world, we declare ourselves feminist counterparts to the mostly male tradition of anonymous do-gooders like Robin Hood, Batman, and the Lone Ranger. We wear gorilla masks to focus on the issues rather than our personalities. The mystery surrounding our identities has attracted attention and support. We could be anyone; we are everywhere."

NrrdGrrl

http://www.nrrdgrrl.com/contents.html

NrrdGrrl! Is the online home for women from around the world who think, talk, and act for themselves. Grrowl! is a quarterly literary magazine for teen writers who want to publish their work. The site offers plenty of back issues available for downloading. NrrdGrrl!

Gallery is a gallery of women who will help girls re-define beauty, attractiveness, and success.

Razzberry

http://www.razzberry.com/home.html

Razzberry is for young women aching to voice their opinions somewhere new. This online forum-based community for female teens will let girls share their ideas, listen to and support each other, open their minds, and let their opinions be known—the good ones or, especially, the bad.

Teen Voices

http://www.teenvoices.com/

Let girls know they're more than just another pretty face! This quarterly magazine helps girls unlock their hidden potential by encouraging them to be themselves. It features original writing, poetry, artwork, and relevant articles that deal with the issues that teenage girls face every day.

Freebies

If you think you're free, there's no escape possible.
– Ram Dass

Free Shop

http://www.freeshop.com/

You couldn't ask for a better freebie site if you paid for one. FreeShop offers hundreds of free and trial offers from hundreds of nationally recognized advertisers so your teens can "try before they buy." And, once your teen is in the buyers market, they can even use their shopping assistant to compare prices across the Internet.

The Free Site

http://www.thefreesite.com/

Nothing is better than "free," and this site knows it. Home to some of the best of the Web's freebies, the Free Site offers almost every sound, game, product sample, screen saver, Web space, and more that's available for free on the Net. It even offers a newsletter to keep surfers in the know about the latest freebies—which, of course, is also free.

Free WWW Resources at the Free Well

http://www.icemall.com/free/free_sites.html

Free is this site's middle name. More than just a place to discover free products on the Net, Icemall will link your teen to free business opportunities, e-mail, adver-tising, classifieds, books, marketing, reports, programming, and just about anything that a teen could ever want (and don't want to pay for). Simply use the search engine to find it in a snap.

freebies, freebies, freebies and more freebies

http://www.geocities.com/siliconvalley/1055/free.html

Many teens may really enjoy this personal homepage of freebies that, while not competing with the big boys, can offer some rare and unique freebies-such as puppy care kits and beanie babies, as well as the usual free tee shirts, contests, e-mail, and sample products. However, be aware that many of the free offers listed here may be outdated.

Freestuff, Freebies, free, free samples—Free2b's Fantastic Freebies

http://www.free2bs.com/

If it's available on the Net for free, teens can find it here. This site goes to great lengths to find the latest freebies on the Web, and it posts them daily on their website. The articles range from free phone minutes and tee shirts to cookie cutters. They include links to contests, free graphics, and recipes. Sponsored by Free2b's Fantastic Freebies.

100% Freebies

http://www.all-movies.com/freebies/

This is great selection of many free offers, free subscriptions, more freebie sites, sweepstakes, contests, and giveaways. Teens can use it to check out the Top 50 Freebie Sites or join the monthly online newsletter—for free, of course. By clicking on Catalogues, typing in their e-mail address, and answering some quick questions about their interests, they can have truckloads of catalogues delivered to their mailbox.

Full-Text Resources

There are worse crimes than burning books. One of them is not reading them. – Joseph Brodsky

BiblioBytes

http://www.bb.com/

BiblioBytes archives hundreds of electronic texts available for free download. Browse by title, author, category/genre, even text string, or review the entire (lengthy) catalog; other features include submittal guidelines and a "banned books" archive.

1st Books Library

http://www.1stbooks.com/

1st Books Library offers more than 2,000 electronic books, including hundreds at no cost, arranged in archives by literary genre and book type, and searchable by title and author. This site also previews forthcoming additions to their collection.

Project Gutenberg

http://www.promo.net/pg/

Project Gutenberg presents an overview of this initiative to bring classic literature into the digital age. Browse by author or title in alphabetical order.

Works of the Bard

http://www.gh.cs.usyd.edu.au/~matty/Shakespeare/

This site is a complete virtual library dedicated solely to William Shakespeare. Students will find links to complete electronic text versions of every one of Shakespeare's works. The site is divided into sections on the histories, poetry, comedies and tragedies, plus a helpful glossary and a section on other Web resources related to Shakespeare.

Games

Some people seem to go through life standing at the complaint counter. – Fred Propp Jr.

Acorn Gaming

http://www.acorn-gaming.org.uk/

This site features reviews of recent game releases, details of forthcoming games, and related Mac news. Links are highlighted.

The Adrenaline Vault

http://www.avault.com/

This is a comprehensive e-zine for gamers that features a variety of gaming news, including previews and new releases. It also offers downloads of selected games, reviews and previews, articles and editorials, cheats and hints, giveaways and forums.

Aerodrome.org

http://www.teleport.com/~belagus/index.html

If teens are really interested in vintage air simulations, such as Microsoft's Flight-Sim 98 and Combat Flight Sim, and Dynamix's Red Baron, this site will be a wonderful resource for them.

All Games Network

http://www.allgames.com/

Teens who are up to their ears in games will find the latest information on games like Fantasy Football, Thunk! Game Show, Professional Gamers League, Pseudo Romance, Streetsound, and Pseudo Sports at this site.

Atomic Games

http://atomic.com/

New game releases are the specialty of this site, notably Close Combat 3. Some of the releases are available for download. An unusual feature is a section on career opportunities for interested gamers. Sponsored by Atomic Games, a privately held game company in Texas.

AutoSim World Records Site

http://www.379.com/aswrs/

The gamer can use this site to locate the all-time greatest scores for popular PC racing simulations such as Need for Speed, Rally Championship, and SODA Off-Road Racing.

Cheat Planet--Planet PC!

http://www.cheatplanet.com/pcplanet.html

Cheat Planet, aka The Planet's Best Cheat Codes, offers cheats, codes, and game guides to select PC titles popular with teens. It also includes dates of the latest and the greatest releases and free game downloads.

Flight Simulator Forum

http://www.delphi.com/flight/

Do your teens like to fly via modem? Have them check out this database of other pilots, and find a partner. This site offers a look at the latest flight simulator phenom to hit the market shelves. Is it a boom or a bust? Join in the conversation on this new topic in the Forum.

FlightSim.Com

http://www.flightsim.com/

FlightSim offers teens a wide assortment of flight-simulation resources, including civilian and military forums, FAQs, reviews, and developer information.

Game World

http://www.geocities.com/TimesSquare/Arcade/
9575/

Teen gamers can skim the news on popular and just
released computer games or view a listing of ezines and
links to game developers at this information site.

GamePen

http://www.gamepen.com:80/

Fans can compare a wide variety of different types of
games at this site. Categories include action, adventure,
flight simulations, and strategy/war. Game previewing
is available.

Games Domain

http://www.gamesdomain.co.uk/directd/directd.html

One of the premiere game sites on the Web, surfers can
get demos, downloads, online games, cheats, patches,
walkthroughs, charts, and freebies. Updates of new
games are added daily. Resources for gaming enthusiasts
include game FAQs, hardware, and company information
for players. Sponsored by Games Domain.

GameSpot

http://www.gamespot.com

Gamers can obtain access to a gigantic selection of the
latest computer game demos, reviews, and hints
through this site. GameSpot takes gaming one step
further than most other game sites by offering computer tips to improve game playing and the opportunity to
be a beta-tester. Sponsored by GameSpot Inc.

GameSpot's Software Library

http://shareware.gamespot.com/index.html

If your teens are looking for a variety of classic arcade
games packed with action, adventure, role playing,
puzzles, logic, simulation, sports, strategy, and war
games, or they want the latest board, card, casino, and
word games, this is the place to visit.

GameWeb – Top 50

http://thegw.com/top50.html

Teens can access 50 game sites ranked by category. The
site offers links to actual games, and provides downloading opportunities. Teen gamers should peruse the
cheats archive and the gaming site of the week.

Happy Puppy

http://www.happypuppy.com

Happy Puppy is a game-player's heaven. This gaming
clearinghouse holds the world's largest collection of

online and computer game demos, freeware, shareware,
and reviews. Just click through their easy-to-navigate
categories and download to start playing in minutes.
The site also includes hints, cheats, bulletin boards and
chat rooms to keep in touch with the gaming world.
Sponsored by Attitude Network, Ltd.

Jumbo! Games

http://www.jumbo.com/pages/games/

Games, games and more games!!! Your teens can
download over 23,000 games and demos at this site
and the number is growing rapidly. They can sign up
for a free newsletter to receive special offers on products, search Jumbo's gigantic database, or tune into
channels like hobbies, homework, internet, kids, lotto,
music, postcards, screen savers, starter kits, theme park
and upload central. Sponsored by Jumbo.

MVP Software: Free Game Downloads

http://www.mvpsoft.com/download_shareware.html

MVP is for shareware users. The site offers extensive
graphics and extended playing times. Action, adventure,
card, and word games are highlighted.

Motorsports Mania

http://www.geocities.com/MotorCity/Track/6704/

Everything a young person always wanted to know about
motor sports racing can be found at this site. They can
check out the Grand Prix legends, Internet racing, hardware tests, links page, and monthly news. They can also
join an online racing league and race with other enthusiasts across the globe. Sponsored by Mark Reynolds

Nintendo Sports

http://www.nintendosports.com/

This is the official site dedicated to Nintendo 64's
sports titles. Fans can find reviews of games, contests,
polls, and interviews with game producers.

Roger's Classic Arcade Tips & Tricks

http://www.classicgaming.com/rcatt/

Teens can get some inside advice on how to improve
their scores and beat over 80 classic video games.

3D Gaming World

http://www.3dgw.com/

If your teens are searching for 3D games, demos, software reviews, patches, previews, release dates, 3D cards,
benchmarks, drivers, hardware reviews, utilities, and
articles, this is the place. All are free and available for
immediate download. Each entry includes a brief

review of the game, download time, and file size. Sponsored by 3D Gaming World.

Tower of Pin

http://www.pcpinball.com/

For the pinball wizard, this is the place for pinball simulations, reviews of pinball games, pinball software, pinball simulation rulesheets, top scores, and the history of pinball. Teens can join the Pinball Club or leave a message on the message board. There's even a database archive with links to outside pinball resources on the web. Sponsored by Jumpgate

Ultisoft.com

http://www.softsite.com/

Arcade games, mindbenders, action games, card games, casino games and more. Play scrolling games, fast action blocks games, and puzzles. There is enough here to satisfy any teen's game playing habit for the entire millennium.

Video Game Heaven.com

http://www.videogameheaven.com/main.htm

This is another website devoted to games and products that are about to be released. It also features reviews and updated news flashes for the gaming industry.

The Video Game Master

http://www.geocities.com/TimesSquare/Alley/3587

Yet another site that offers access to comprehensive game profiles, cheats, and downloads for games like the Command & Conquer series and Diablo.

The Wargamer

http://www.wargamer.com/

For those who are not troubled about war games, this site offers regularly updated news and upgrades/patches for war games, and the top ten downloads.

Geography (See also Travel)

If you're not certain where to go, any road will take you there. – Anonymous

Atlapedia Online

http://www.atlapedia.com/

Atlapedia Online contains full-color physical and political maps as well as key facts and statistics on countries of the world. Students will be surprised how much information this site offers on each country.

Cyberbuss

http://www.cyberbuss.com/index2.htm

Teens interested in geography can take a virtual ride on the Cyberbuss at this site. The Cyberbuss travels to remote places all over the earth. It presumes that national or geographic boundaries have vanished and there are fewer language barriers. It also gives adventuresome young adults the opportunity to be two places at one time.

GLOBIS

http://www.frw.ruu.nl/nicegeo.html

This directory of geography sites will be indispensable for students facing a geography report or test. Many of the sites get to be a bit technical for teen audiences, so parents and teachers need to be selective. However, there are plenty of helpful sites. Sponsored by Utrecht University.

Map Machine

http://www.nationalgeographic.com/resources/ngo/maps

This well-produced site from National Geographic contains a Map Machine Atlas. It gives users access to maps, facts, flags and profiles of the countries, map resources, political maps, physical maps, an expeditions atlas and the "View From Above," which shows satellite imagery of political borders. This view from space enables students to zoom in on a specific country. All they have to do is click on the continent they want to explore.

Project GeoSim

http://geosim.cs.vt.edu

Project GeoSim is a tutorial program designed to introduce geo-political terms and concepts, and a simulation program with which to carry out lab exercises. Human Population is a multimedia tutorial program that illustrates population concepts and issues. Sense of Place focuses on the characteristics of U.S. counties and states. Mental Maps is a geography quiz program. Sponsored by the Departments of Computer Science and Geography at Virginia Tech.

Government

In a democracy everybody has a right to be represented, including the jerks. – Chris Patten

• State and Local

Local Government Institute

http://www.lgi.org/

Dedicated to improving the quality of and participation in municipal oversight, various sections of the Local Government Institute (LGI) home page offer employment, recruitment and consulting services, links to other government resources, and pertinent software and publications.

National Association of State Information Resources Executives

http://www.nasire.org/

The National Association of State Information Resource Executives (NASIRE) presents an expansive archive of minutes from the group's meetings and conferences, awards presented by and to its membership, and related print and digital publications.

State and Local Government on the Net

http://www.piperinfo.com/state/states.html

This site presents an impressive matrix of links to government branches below the federal level. The alphabetic state matrix is supplemented by additional sections featuring federal resources and national organizations.

• United States

CapWeb—A Guide to the U.S.Congress.

http://www.congress.org/

This interesting site permits teens to keep track of the performance of their Congressional Representatives. Congress.org offers a directory of Congress-by state, by Representative, by committee-as well as contact information, an automatic e-mail box for each member, and a Legislative scorecard. This website will also help teens find the legislator who serves their geographic area so they can easily lobby for an issue. Sponsored by Capitol Advantage.

Central Intelligence Agency

http://www.cia.gov/

This is the official website for the Central Intelligence Agency. The mission of the CIA is to provide evidence-based, comprehensive, and timely foreign intelligence related to national security. The CIA also conducts counterintelligence activities, special activities, and other functions related to foreign intelligence and national security as directed by the President. Visitors to this site can learn more about the activities and role of the CIA, and take a virtual tour of the CIA in the nations capital.

Congressional E-mail

http://congress.nw.dc.us/c-span/elecmail.html

This service allows any citizen to communicate with his or her member of Congress. Access is by Zip Code or the representative's name. The site will help the user to compose and send either e-mail or regular mail letters.

Congressional E-Mail Directory

http://www.webslingerz.com/jhoffman/congress-email.html

The Congressional E-Mail Directory provides all citizens with quick access to their elected representative: Each entry in the alphabetic matrix of U.S. states and territories returns a hyperlinked list of representatives, with each name linked to their e-mailbox.

Core Documents of U.S. Democracy

http://www.access.gpo.gov/su_docs/dpos/
    whatcore.html

Get direct access to the basic federal government documents starting with the Articles of Confederation and on through the most recent Supreme Court decisions here. All three branches of the federal government are represented in this collection. Links are provided to electronic versions of all documents. There are additional links to basic governmental reference publications such as the Census and the U.S. Government Manual. Sponsored by the GPO Library Programs Service.

Government Auctions and Surplus Property Sales

http://www.financenet.gov/sales.htm

Part of the FinanceNet initiative for accountability in public fiscal management, this site presents efficiently organized information about items available for sale or government auction, and links to newsgroups and e-mail lists devoted to the subject.

Jobs in Government

http://www.jobsingovernment.com/

Jobs in Government presents an organized database of employment opportunities and options for both employers and potential employees, including a sophisticated search engine, resume bulletin board, and job matrix by location and description.

The Library of Congress

http://lcweb.loc.gov/homepage/lchp.html

One of the most comprehensive library resources in the world, from the Library of Congress home page you can access its monumental holdings in a searchable database, organized into categories for online exhibitions, the Copyright Office, and a multimedia history of America.

Supreme Court Decisions

http://supct.law.cornell.edu/supct/

The Supreme Court Collection, developed by the Legal Information Institute, provides details on more than 600 of the Court's most historic decisions. It is cross-referenced both chronologically and by topic, and it is searchable by keyword.

Understanding the Federal Courts

http://www.uscourts.gov/understanding_courts/899 _toc.htm

Understanding the Federal Courts spares the graphics and layout but not the information, offering intricate descriptions of the Supreme Court and the U.S. Court of Appeals, plus directories of U.S. District and Appeals Courts.

United States Census Bureau

http://www.census.gov/

The home page for the U.S. Census Bureau provides statistical data and other information about American life, divided into categories for people, geography and business, plus a news section and separate databases for each state.

White House

http://www.whitehouse.gov/

Home page for the White House, this site has the expected information about the presidency and current topics of national interest. It also provides a good launching place for other commonly requested federal services.

White House Press Releases, Speeches and Other Documents

http://www.vote-smart.org/executive/presspe.htm

Project Vote Smart provides an archive of daily press releases, press briefings, Executive Orders, weekly radio address transcripts, and other White House communications, all in a topically searchable database.

Grammar and Style Guides

Everything yields to success. Even grammar.
– Victor Hugo

Elements of Style

http://www.bartleby.com/141/index.html

This guide to grammar rules and written style is the online version of the perennial classic. Students can use the alphabetized table of contents to find specific rules for proper usage or read the essays for broad discussions of writing style. The site also provides a list of other recommended style guides, and links to other online writers' resources. No student's library should be without a copy—online or otherwise.

Grammar Lady

http://www.grammarlady.com/

The homespun Grammar Lady's site addresses proper grammar and sentence structure with warmth and whimsy. Features include a monthly grammar tip; a schedule of the Grammar Lady's public appearances (mainly radio); and questions, comments, typos and sites of the week. Users can exchange their own information and ideas on several different message boards.

Guide to Grammar and Writing

http://webster.commnet.edu/HP/pages/darling/gra mmar.htm

This writer's guide first discusses the cornerstone of good writing—using the right words in the right order in the right sentence. It also addresses such issues as noun-verb agreement, capitalization, and punctuation. It then progresses from building solid sentences into solid paragraphs, and solid paragraphs into intelligent essays. Features include contests and quizzes associated with writing and grammar, and links to other writing resources.

WordNet

http://www.cogsci.princeton.edu/~wn/

An interactive lexical database for English, WordNet provides an interconnected roadmap through most of the language: nouns, adjectives, verbs and adverbs are organized into sets of synonyms, plus synonyms for different word meanings in different contexts. Students can either use the site, download a free copy, or purchase the software for more extensive use.

Health

You have to stay in shape. My grandmother started walking five miles a day when she was 60. She's 97 today, and we don't know where she is. – Ellen Degeneres

AMA Health Insight

http://www.ama-assn.org/consumer.htm

The American Medical Association sponsors medical, general health and first aid information. Browse the search engines for Specific Conditions, General Health, Family Focus, and Interactive Health.

allhealth.com

http://www.allhealth.com/experts/

Licensed and practicing physicians are available at this site to answer your questions. From alternative medicine to women's health, anyone who logs on can just fire away and the answers will appear.

The Daily Apple

http://thedailyapple.com

Based on the adage that an apple a day keeps the doctor away, teens can get their Daily Apple e-mail newsletter with health news tidbites at this site. They can also search the huge database of information relating to male, female, children's and senior's health issues.

Health Screen America

http://www.GuidetoHealth.com/

This site contains educational handouts, audio clips, slide shows, books, and links on the subjects of Women's Health, Men's Health, Heart Disease and Cancer Prevention.

Medical Ethics: Where Do You Draw the Line?

http://www.learner.org/exhibits/medicalethics/

The variety of new technologies and developments in medicine and health care raise controversial and confusing ethical questions. Teens can learn about current research and explore their own beliefs about these new issues. Great resource for debate information.

OnLine Surgery

http://www.onlinesurgery.com/

Students can watch live surgery over the Internet. Past procedures can be viewed in the surgery archives. They can also find a surgeon in the Surgeon Finder database.

A Patient's Guide to the Internet

http://www.patientsguide.com

This is a thorough, step-by-step guide, with over 20,000 medical sites to browse, for patients seeking any type of medical information. Students can access research, references, resources, support groups, medical terminology, and a glossary of medical terms. Subscribes to the HONcode of conduct for medical and health websites.

The Physician Advisor

http://www.phys-advisor.com

This site will help teens answer popular medical questions about supplements such as DHEA and melatonin, how to select a physician, how to review and evaluate medical insurance plans, how to find information in the medical literature, what is safe weight loss, and more. This site is designed to empower the lay public to make informed decisions regarding their health, not replace a physicians advice.

Wellness Guide

http://niazi.com/Wellness%20Guide/frames42.htm

This is a great health e-zine with articles on health tips about nutrition, exercise, mental health, and more. Teens will find it is well organized and easy to navigate.

YourHealth.com

http://YourHealth.com/

Teens will especially enjoy the RealAudio interviews, where they can ask questions before or during the program, and then check the transcripts. The Reference Center contains thousands of articles on a wide range of health topics. Join health experts every night of the week and ask your own health-related questions.

Health--Diseases and Conditions

Be smart, be intelligent and be informed.
– Tony Alesandra

(Because of the variety of information that may be found on these websites, parents, teachers and librarians may wish to visit these sites before referring teens to them.)

• AIDS

AIDS and Young People

http://www.avert.org/young.htm

This site offers up the straight scoop on AIDS (Acquired Immune Deficiency Syndrome) and what teens can do to help prevent it. It even includes a free information booklet by mail. Sponsored by Avert.

AIDS Resource List

http://www.teleport.com/~celinec/aids.shtml

The launch pad to all other AIDS sites. Comprehensive list of AIDS/HIV resources on the Internet, ranging from local to international sites.

Metro Teen AIDS

http://www.metroteenaids.org/

The who, what, where, and why of teen AIDS. This site reinforces the viewpoint that a teenager's best defense is to be informed, and here, they can become well armed with facts, advice, information on testing facilities, support centers, and ways that they can get involved and make a difference in the fight against HIV/AIDS.

Teen AIDS Peercorps

http://www.teenaids-peercorps.com/

What every teen should know about AIDS and HIV—offered in almost every language! This site reinforces that it's not who you are, but what you do that matters in transmitting this deadly disease. Includes advice columns, forums, facts, tips, Harvard research findings, and even art. Sponsored by TeenAIDS-Peercorps Inc.

• Allergies

AllerDays

http://www.allerdays.com/

Exclusively featuring allergy information from hayfever/allergic rhinitis, allergic reactions, allergists, allergens, pollen forecasts to advice on medications, treatments, and answers to your questions.

Food Allergy Network

http://www.foodallergy.org/

FAN educates consumers, health professionals and reporters about food allergies, product alerts, recalls of foods, allergy conscious recipes, and food allergy research.

Resources for People with Food Allergies & Intolerances

http://www.skyisland.com/OnlineResources/

Hundreds of tried and true wheat-free, egg-free, milk-free recipes. A forum designed for disseminating information about food resources, food additives information, links and more.

• Cancer

Cancer Information and Support International

http://www.cancer-info.com

A plain, but helpful site specific to cancer. Students can get information about traditional, conventional, and natural treatments, spiritual awareness and healing, recipes for longevity, recipes from visitors, news in research, and the latest breakthroughs.

Cancer Resources

http://www.ianr.unl.edu/pubs/health/nf325.htm

Patients, family members, support groups and health professionals can access a large quantity of current cancer information at this site.

OncoLink

http://www.oncolink.upenn.edu/

The University of Pennsylvania Cancer Center offers invaluable information on the causes of cancer, prevention, faqs, support, clinical trials, and much more.

• Chronic Illness

The Bearable Times: Kids & Teens Club

http://www.bearabletimes.org/

Created by the Kids' Hospital Network, this site caters to children who are ill or have health challenges, offering them enjoyable activities, support, and resources to get them back in the swing of things. The site includes a chat room, classroom projects, homework helpers, online games, homepages, exercises, recipes, and fun and interesting links—everything to make staying at home or the hospital bearable.

ChronicIllnet

http://www.chronicillnet.org/

For anyone who suffers from a chronic illness, this site offers abstracts on groundbreaking research, bulletin boards, events calendars, guest lectures, and news articles in the Community section.

National Institute of Diabetes

http://www.niddk.nih.gov/

This is the official site for the National Institute of Diabetes and Digestive and Kidney Diseases. Teens can find accurate and extensive information on the most serious diseases affecting public health, educational programs and materials, and news releases on the latest research findings and activities.

• Eating Disorders

Eating Disorders

http://www.mirror-mirror.org/eatdis.htm

Young people will appreciate this informative site that includes definitions of common medical terms, signs of eating disorders, symptoms, where to get help, how to help a friend or relative with an eating disorder, and a wealth of data to aid in developing a term paper on this subject.

Something Fishy: Website on Eating Disorders

http://www.something-fishy.org/

This youth-oriented website is devoted to raising awareness and providing online support for anyone suffering from an eating disorder. The comforting message "You are not alone" reverberates throughout the site. Something Fishy is an organization "working to help stop the voices." Learn the signs and symptoms of anorexia, bulimia, and overeating, what you can do to help family members and friends, and get tips for parents and doctors. Teens can also chat with others struggling with these issues.

Teens and Eating Disorders

http://www.mirror-mirror.org/teens.htm

Everything your teens ever need to know about anorexia, bulimia, and compulsive overeating can be found here, including how to prevent and stop the occurrence or eating disorders. From the whys and hows to the where to go for help, this site offers it all in easy reference categories.

• Stuttering

Just for Teens: For Teens Who Stutter

http://www.mankato.msus.edu/dept/comdis/kuster/kids/teens.html

This information-packed site can boost the morale of teens who stutter by letting them know they're not alone. It offers non-stutters a rare insight to the world of stuttering, and it features facts and books about stut-

tering, personal accounts from teens who suffer from stuttering. You'll be surprised by the list of famous people who stutter.

Health--Dental

A man's palate can, in time, become accustomed to anything. – Napoleon Bonaparte

Teen Orthodonture

http://www.bracesinfo.com/teenage.html

This site explains why some people need braces, how orthodontic treatment works, what it is like to have braces, the different kinds of braces, and what steps occur during orthodontic treatment. A wacky cast of characters turns a plain site into an animated story. FradyCat is a patient who is afraid of braces. Cool Dude tells kids how to be cool with braces. Guy Funi is a guy who knows how to have fun in braces. Dr. Bob is a friendly orthodontist who will give viewers the official answers. Professor Hatt, DMD, will answer the really hard questions.

The Tooth Fairy

http://www.toothfairy.org/

With a motto like "Be true to your teeth or they'll be false to you," this site is guaranteed to have plenty of good dental tips and resources for teens.

Health--Directories

Advice is what we ask for when we already know the answer but wish we didn't. – Erica Jong

Essential Links to Medical Information

http://www.EL.com/

This site is a guide to the essential resources about medicine, medical information, facilities, diseases, hospitals, organizations, and other health-related issues on the Internet.

Guide to Medical Information and Support on the Internet

http://www.geocities.com/HotSprings/1505/guide.html

Although the Internet has revolutionized health care, it contains so much information that it is very difficult for young people to get to the heart of their medical concerns. Have them start here!

Health Care Information Resources on the Web

http://www.xnet.com/~hret/statind.htm

Teens can download a wealth of interesting health reports, and check out the links to federal, state and local health information.

Health Clinic USA

http://www.familyinternet.com/healthclinicusa/
  index.html

Young people can use the Family Internet website to find information on diseases, injury, poison, tests, drugs, and diets. There is also a huge database that provides links on diseases from A-Z, starting with arthritis and covering all of the major conditions.

Health Network.com

http://www.healthwave.com/

A significant health and medicine Web directory and search engine designed to be used for research to empower and inform.

HealthNews.com

http://www.healthnewsdirectory.com/

This website offers teens a comprehensive and well researched health and medical news directory. Each category lists related links and current articles.

How to Search for Medical Information

http://204.17.98.73/midlib/www.htm

Consumers and health professionals will discover how to take charge of their own health care by searching for medical information on the Web. Orientation to the Web environment, specific diseases, drugs and treatments, medical statistics, medicine in the news, and doctors credentials all serve as an online tutorial to Web health information research.

MEDguide

http://www.avicom.net/medguide/

Teens interested in a career in health service will find valuable information in this guide to health care and medical resources on the Internet. Includes links to institutes, organizations, medical specialities, hospitals, and medical colleges.

Medical Access Online

http://www.medical-access.com/index.html/

All ages will appreciate this directory of links to physicians, healthcare discussion boards, professional organizations, hospitals, disease and health information, medical products guide, physician sites, and more. Sponsored by Medical Access Online.

Mediconsult.com

http://www.mediconsult.com

This is a tremendous source of information and services for health care consumers. In the "Pick a Condition" section, teens can select from a list of over 80 diseases to get detailed definitions, symptoms, medications and treatment plans. They can also perform a search through medical journals to read about clinical studies and findings pertaining to specific conditions.

Medline Fool!

http://www.medportal.com/

When researching health-related issues the National Library of Medicine's comprehensive database is an outstanding launching pad for the latest medical journal information. This site includes an extensive index and search engine to other Web sources.

WebDoctor

http://www.gretmar.com/webdoctor/window.html

Although this site was primarily designed by physicians, for physicians, this is a resource that might be of interest to older teens who are serious about advancing their medical knowledge. Each site is reviewed by physicians before it is listed. WebDoctor contains over 10,000 documents.

Health--Diet & Nutrition (*See also* Physical Fitness)

It takes more than just a good looking body. You've got to have the heart and soul to go with it. – Lee Haney

AVA Health

http://www.lhsusa.com/

This online health foods store claims to offer over 3,000 health, fitness, and beauty products in its online catalog. Shoppers can take advantage of discounted specials, obtain information about new products, supplements and releases.

America's Top 6 Fad Diets

http://homearts.com:80/gh/health/07nutrf1.htm

Many teens are attracted to the promise of easy and quick weight loss that many fad diets offer. This article from the *Good Housekeeping Magazine* debunks the six most popular diet fads. Sound advice is offered on how to lose weight in a healthy fashion, and on preparing more nutritious meals.

The Boys Health and Nutrition Program

http://www.bostonchildhealth.org/projecthealth/
bfn.phtml

This program provides an opportunity for boys ages 10 to 12 who are at risk for being overweight or obese to participate in a variety of fitness activities, explore improved nutrition, and benefit from both mentoring and peer support as they work to change lifestyle habits.

Calorie Calculator

http://homearts.com/helpers/calculators/calcalc.htm

A handy resource for anyone who wants to stay healthy. The calorie calculator gives the precise number of calories a person should be eating each day by entering their weight and level of activity. It also provides information on the calories that will be burned up by certain activities and exercises.

Diet & Weight Loss/Fitness

http://www1.mhv.net/~donn/diet.html

Health lovers will find a great selection of articles and links to diet tips, exercise, low fat recipes, diet news, support, FAQs, reviews of new weight loss products, and nutrition at this URL. Site by Health Vision.

Diettalk.com

http://www.diettalk.com

A wide range of links to resources on weight loss, diet programs, and calorie calculators. Ask the Dietitian, a file on eating disorders, recommended diet magazines, recipes, software, and a chat room are also included.

Health and Weight Loss

http://www.Comsource.net/~bwelch/health_and_
weight_loss.html

This page will provide information on how to calculate body fat and determine basal metabolic rate. It also provides advice on recommended vitamins and minerals that aid in weight loss.

LEARN Education Center

http://www.learneducation.com

It doesn't take a rocket scientist to understand that stress contributes to poor diet. This site offers recommendations on controlling and reducing stress, as well as improving diet and exercise. There are articles by experts and links to other related sites.

Weight Management

http://external.aomc.org/HOD2/general/weight-
Contents.html

Visitors to this site will find a searchable database containing information on weight management. Departments include obesity, recipes, exercise, advice on food choices, and tips for successful dieting. Sponsored by the Arnot Ogden Medical Center.

Health--First Aid

Well done is quickly done. – Augustus Caesar

First Aid

http://www.mayohealth.org/mayo/library/htm/
firstaid.htm

This resource from the Mayo Clinic is designed to provide basic first aid information on the most common injuries. Users can learn how to treat bumps and bruises to bee stings, shock and trauma, and when to call a doctor.

PARASOL EMT: First Aid

http://www.parasolemt.com.au/

What would you do in a life threatening emergency? This site offers guidance in what to do, how to react, and what is needed in emergencies. Features include online CPR and EAR training, how to stop bleeding, how to handle sports injuries, body trauma and venomous bites and stings.

Health--Mental Health

There are four ways, and only four ways, in which we have contact with the world. We are evaluated and classified by these four contacts: what we do, how we look, what we say, and how we say it. – Dale Carnegie

allaboutcounseling.com

www.allaboutcounseling.com

Who doesn't need the chance to express themselves, ask questions, solve seemingly unsolvable problems and vent about everyday struggles? This site gives teens that opportunity. It contains resources for professional counselors, links to other counseling sites and periodic online discussions.

Psych Web

www.psychwww.com

Ever tried to figure out what that strange dream you keep having means? Psych Web is a directory of psychology related information for students to help them interpret their dreams. It offers full-length classics online such as *The Interpretation of Dreams* by Sigmund Freud, information on careers in psychology, online pamphlets, journals, and megalists of psychology-related websites. Sponsored by Russell A. Dewey, Ph.D.

Health--Teen

You are only young once, and if you work it right, once is enough. – Joe E. Lewis

ADOL: Adolescence Directory On-Line

http://education.indiana.edu/cas/adol/adol.html

Adolescence Directory On-Line (ADOL) is an electronic guide to information on adolescent issues. It is a service of the Center for Adolescent Studies at Indiana University. Educators, counselors, parents, researchers, health practitioners, and teens can use ADOL to find Web resources on hard-hitting topics. For mature audiences only. Sponsored by the Indiana University Center for Adolescent Studies.

Face Facts

http://www.facefacts.com/

Not too many teens escape the joys of acne. Roche, a leader in dermatology, offers good advice so teens can learn how to avoid or reduce skin disorders. It debunks the popular myths on acne, and offers the straight facts, explanations of the medical terms, and the know-how to become an acne expert. Additional teen links and mailing addresses for further information are listed.

GirlSpace

http://www.girlspace.com

This is a well-designed site to help girls, parents, and teachers take the embarrassment and mystery out of a girl's menstrual cycle. It offers clear facts about periods, tips on keeping girls' bodies healthy, informative quizzes, and a place for girls to hang, vent, share, talk, and yell. Sponsored by Kotex.

Go Ask Alice

http://www.goaskalice.columbia.edu/index.html

Columbia University sponsors this terrific site about health topics for mature teens. It is graphically intense and beautifully produced. The sections are New Alice Questions, Relationships, Sexuality, Sexual Health, Emotional Health, Fitness and Nutrition, and Alcohol, Nicotine & Other Drugs. The site has three outstanding features:1) New Alice! Q&As of the Week gives teens the latest inquiries and responses with weekly updates. 2) Search Alice! lets teens find health information by subject via a search of the Go Ask Alice! Archives containing thousands previously-posted questions and answers. 3) Ask Alice! gives teens the chance to ask Alice a question.

Is Your Period a Question Mark?

http://www.troom.com/calendar/calendar.html

A site just for preteen and teen girls to help them understand and follow their menstruation cycle. Here, girls can chart their cycle using an online calendar to determine when their period will occur. It is especially helpful for girls who need to see if they're regular or irregular to determine if they should see a doctor about it.

On the Teen Scene

http://www.fda.gov/opacom/7teens.html

This FDA consumer magazine periodically runs articles with important health information for teenagers, ranging from nutrition and sun safety to eating disorders and attention deficit disorder. These "Teen Scene" articles are archived electronically.

Puberty 101

http://www.virtualkid.com/p101/p101_menu.shtml

Puberty 101 was started by J. Geoff Malta, MA, EdM, NCC, an adolescent therapist. It offers a place on the Web for adolescents and teens to ask questions and get honest open answers about puberty. VirtualKid Teen is the sponsor.

Sex. Etc.

http://www.sxetc.org/

The Network for Family Life Education has produced an award-winning site for teens about sexuality. It covers a range of topics that include Abstinence, Condoms and Birth Control, Gay and Lesbian teens,

Love and Dating, Pregnancy and Parenting, and Violence and Abuse. Subscribe to the free e-mail newsletter that features timely articles. The purpose of the newspaper and the online version is to "give teens a place to go in cyberspace where they could get accurate, up-front information about their sexuality. This also gives teens a place to get their questions answered. Much of the information is written by teens. Sponsored by Rutgers University.

Teen Health and the Media

http://depts.washington.edu/ecttp/default.html

This virtual meeting place for teens offers a 24-hour crisis hotline and accurate information on teen health, sexuality, violence, suicide, drug use, and media literacy. Sponsored by the Early Childhood Teen/ Telecommunications Project.

Teen Talk: Health

http://www.teentalk.com

This is another popular website that offers easily understood facts on teen health, sexuality, school, careers, relationships, parents, and just about anything affecting a teen's life. All topics feature honest discussion, questions and answers. The basic concept is that one can learn a lot by sharing in the joys and hardships of others. CyberMom sponsors this site.

Health--Women

The trouble with some women is they get all excited about nothing, and then they marry him. – Cher

Estronaut

http://www.womenshealth.org/

Facts, information, advice, and suggestions are offered to help teen girls deal with their health concerns. Articles are designed, written, and developed by a woman physician and other women's health professionals.

Health Source

http://www.thehealthsource.com

The key features of this site are animations, factual information, discussion groups, news, and health alert e-mail updates on topics from pregnancy to menopause.

National Women's Health Information Center

http://www.4woman.org

This cornucopia of women's health resources and materials designed for healthcare consumers and professionals. It includes a listing of online dictionaries and medical journals, reference sources, databases and print directories and lists.

WomenCare

http://www.womencare.com/

Young people who are seeking a well-organized guide to understanding the effects of PMS, fertility, and osteoporosis, and other major disorders, including breast cancer, stroke, and heart disease will appreciate this resource.

Women's Health Center

http://www.healthy.net/womenshealth

An alternative health resource on natural approaches to women's health, including herbal medicine, nutrition, homeopathy, and Chinese medicine.

Women's Health Interactive

http://www.womens-health.com/

This is a helpful site where young women can learn to take charge of their health care. It offers learning modules for a variety of specialties like gynecology, heart disease, infertility, nutrition, and personal development.

Women's Health Place

http://women.shn.net/index.html

Young adult women will find helpful articles with advice on self care. Search the database, browse the library, chat and leave messages on the bulletin boards.

History--United States (*See also* Museums)

Fellow citizens, we cannot escape history. – Abraham Lincoln

American Memory

http://memory.loc.gov/

Sponsored by the Library of Congress, the American Memory website provides a wealth of primary source and archival material relating to American culture and history. It currently contains over 70 collections online in over a dozen categories ranging from art and architecture to technology and applied sciences. The repository contains manuscripts, printed texts, maps, motion pictures, photographs, prints and sound recordings. An invaluable resource for history and American culture students.

American Studies Web

http://www.georgetown.edu/crossroads/asw/

American Studies covers economy and politics, race and ethnicity, gender and sexuality, literature and hypertext, philosophy and religion, art and material culture, performance and broadcasting, sociology and demography, region and environment, historical and archival resources, as well as current events. This site provides access to a wide selection of resources in these categories. Created by David Phillips.

Betsy Ross Home Page

http://www.libertynet.org/iha/betsy/index.html

Everything a student needs to know about the history of the American flag. Managed by the Independence Hall Association, this site provides a resource on the life of Betsy Ross and the history of American flag. It includes Ross' life story and a virtual tour of her home, plus a photo history of the American flag, proper flag handling procedures, and famous quotes and notes about its history.

Colonial Hall: Biographies of America's Founding Fathers

http://www.colonialhall.com/index.asp

Teachers who are looking for a good resource for American history assignments will want to guide their teens to this site. Colonial Hall offers biographies of the men who signed the Declaration of Independence and other American forefathers, with information reprinted from Goodrich's famous book Lives of the Signers to the Declaration of Independence, published in 1829. The subjects are categorized by state; and there is keyword search capability to locate a particular topic.

Colonial Williamsburg Foundation

http://www.history.org/

Colonial Williamsburg is an increasingly popular destination for senior class visits and family vacations. This website will help to prepare teens and their parents for a visit. It offers a preview of Williamsburg's history, archeology and architecture.

Eighteenth-Century Resources

http://www.andromeda.rutgers.edu

This is a nice compilation of links to resources about 18th century history for students. It covers every cultural and political aspect of the era from gardening and architecture to science and mathematics. Supplemental links for more serious students include discussion groups, academic societies, journals, and home pages for other scholars of this period.

1492: An Ongoing Voyage

http://sunsite.unc.edu/expo/1492.exhibit/Intro.html

Most history textbooks cite 1492 as the year that America was discovered. This website compiles facts that show there were millions of people living in America in 1492. Some scholars believe that for most of the thousands of years before 1492, the peoples living in America weren't even aware of each other. This site features an online exhibition of the early life of the American people, European explorers, conquerors, and settlers. Sponsored by the Library of Congress.

From Revolution to Reconstruction

http://odur.let.rug.nl/~welling/usa/usa.html

American students will see U.S. history from an entirely new perspective once they have been here. Developed by a group of German college students from the University of Groningen, this virtual tour traces the history of Early America and continues on sequentially through the Reconstruction period.

History Matters

http://historymatters.gmu.edu/

Why do we have to study history? Sponsored by George Mason University and City University of New York, this is an annotated list of the best sites on United States history. Articles and resources that link the past to the present help teens understand "why they have to study history." An innovative section called Talking History lets students and teachers participate in discussions with prominent scholars and teachers on teaching American history.

National Civil Rights Museum Virtual Tour

http://www.mecca.org/~crights/cyber.html

Starting with the Brown vs. Board of Education of Topeka, this virtual tour will take students through the important events of civil rights movement. The Montgomery bus boycott, the freedom rides, the Birmingham demonstrations, Freedom Summer, the

March Against Fear, the work of Dr. Martin Luther King, Jr., Little Rock, the student sit-ins, the battle for Ole Miss, the march on Washington, Selma and Montgomery, and the events in Chicago and Memphis. "The Struggle Continues" chronicles this very important period in American History.

1968: The Whole World Was Watching

http://www.stg.brown.edu/projects/1968/

Transcripts, audio recordings, and edited stories of a series of interviews and recollections of the year 1968. Stories about the Vietnam War, the struggle for civil rights, the assassinations of Martin Luther King, Jr. and Robert Kennedy become a living history of one of the most tumultuous years in United States history. Sponsored by the Rhode Island Committee for the Humanities and NetTech: the Northeast Regional Technology in Education Consortium.

Revolutionary War

www.revwar.com

Resplendent in red, white and blue, this site lists an extensive selection of links to informational and commercial sites and other resources offering materials about the American Revolutionary War. Students post on the message board, get information from newsgroups; chat with war re-enactors, and then visit their websites. Collectors can post items wanted or offered for purchase in the classified ads.

Slave Voices

http://scriptorium.lib.duke.edu/slavery/

This site is home to the exhibit "Third Person, First Person: Slave Voices from the Special Collections Library," and it offers young people an up close and personal opportunity to examine the life experiences of American slaves. The exhibit showcases rare materials that document the ambitions, motivations, and struggles of an enslaved people. Memorable and poignant stories are told about these people who were often given no other voice. Sponsored by Duke University.

Smithsonian Institution

http://www.si.edu/

The Smithsonian is a "family" of special museums and galleries, and a visit to its website offers a description and links to each member of the family. Additional features include a search engine that offers access by name and subject, a summary of educational resources for teachers and students, publications and research activities.

This Day in History

http://www.historychannel.com/thisday/

Sponsored by television's "The History Channel," this site features news items, articles and essays, and images and video clips that address "This Day in History." It also offers special interest features on "This Day" in automotive, Wall Street, and Civil War history. Teens can search for a particular topic (or find out what happened on their birthday).

The Vietnam Veterans Home Page

http://grunt.space.swri.edu

The purpose of this site is to honor Vietnam veterans, living and dead, who served their country. The mission of this website is to provide an interactive, online forum for Vietnam veterans, their families and friends. Users can exchange information, stories, poems, songs, art, pictures, and experiences. Teens seeking information on the Vietnam War will find the "Tributes to the Vietnam Veterans" are particularly moving. They reflect the pain and confusion surrounding the Vietnam War. Sponsored by Bill McBride and Federal Express.

History--World

One of the lessons of history is that nothing is often a good thing to do and always a clever thing to say.
– William J. Durant

Ancient World Web

http://www.julen.net/aw/

An invaluable homework resource for teens seeking facts on ancient civilizations. They can browse modern indices linking to sites about celebrated and obscure ancient civilizations, including virtual historical museum exhibits, related college and university academic departments, ancient food recipes, research bibliographies and more. Resources are cross-referenced alphabetically, by geographic region and by subject; the site also features a keyword search engine.

Books and Websites about the Holocaust for Young Adults

http://www.euronet.nl/users/jubo/holocaust.html

This is a touching and powerful tribute to all those who perished in the horror of the Holocaust during World War II. It introduces some of the major books and websites dealing with the stage of world history. This site is primarily devoted to keeping the memory alive so that teens today will have the power and courage to stand up and speak out against hate that occurs in their own lives every day.

The British Museum

http://www.british-museum.ac.uk/

Founded in 1753, the British Museum is part museum, part library, and part educational institution. Its website will provide visitors with access to information about the collections on display, lectures, educational resources for teachers, news releases, schedules of forthcoming events, and a great deal more.

Cybrary of the Holocaust

http://remember.org/

The Cybrary of the Holocaust uses art, discussion groups, photos, poems, and facts to preserve memories and to teach the Holocaust. The Cybrary is organized into 2 sections: Research, areas where you can explore the issues of the Holocaust; and Forums, where discussion is held. The Holocaust Quilt is where people can leave a memory of a victim or survivor of the Holocaust. Created by Michael Declann Dunn.

Distinguished Women of Past and Present

http://www.netsrq.com/~dbois/

Distinguished women who were writers, educators, scientists, heads of state, politicians, civil rights crusaders, artists, entertainers have two things in common. They have made significant contributions to humankind and they are women. Helen Keller, Florence Nightingale, Mother Theresa, Harriet Tubman are just a few of the many women represented here. Search for the biographies by the name, field of activity or chronologically. Sponsored by Danuta Bois.

E-HAWK

http://www.kcdata.com/~ehawk/

If teens like to study military history, have them click this URL. The website will revolutionize students' ideas about martial history. They can subscribe free to the E-HAWK Journal, a military history journal, or look at the World War I Document Archive. This is international in focus, and it presents primary documents about the Great War in one location. The site was developed by the Military Conflict Institute to foster public understanding of the nature of military conflict. Sponsored by Harcourt Brace Publications.

Exploring Ancient World Cultures

http://eawc.evansville.edu/index.htm

This site contains valuable research information on the ancient cultures of the Near East, Egypt, India, China, Greece, Rome, Europe and Islam. Students will find comprehensive hyperlinked essays and chronologies that examine the myriad aspects of these historical civilizations, specifically their literature and art. Funded by grants from the University of Evansville.

Gateway to World History

http://www.hartford-hwp.com/gateway/index.html

Stunning in its complexity and organization, this site compiles links to resources for the study of nearly every aspect of world history, including: history discussion lists; college and university history departments; search utilities on history; images and e-texts organized into categories for Asia, the Americas, Europe and Africa; and the World History Association. Appropriate for more advanced students.

The Great War

http://www.pbs.org/greatwar/

The Great War is a multimedia production that incorporates television, online and print media to explore the history and effect of World War I. "The Great War and the Shaping of the 20th Century" television series went beyond the military and political history of World War I to reveal its ongoing social, cultural and personal impact. Sponsored by KCET/Los Angeles and the BBC in association with the Imperial War Museum of London.

The History Channel Classroom

http://www.historychannel.com/classroom/classroom.html

The History Channel has produced a beautiful site that features the "Best Search in History". Just choose a keyword and dozens of appropriate sites will appear. A search of the word "World War I" brought up great sites on World War I as well as a section called Related People, Related Historical Places, Related Web Sites and related Videos. The organization, content and quality of this site should make it a teen favorite. Sponsored by A& E Television Network.

History Place

http://www.historyplace.com/

A very well done website on World History provides a great starting point for research papers, lesson plans and timelines. The writing is clear and easy to understand, unlike some textbooks. Contains a section of books appropriate for that topic of study.

History Timelines

http://www.search-beat.com/history.htm

Teens can travel through history with a click of the mouse using this well-organized and extensive list of historical resources from around the Net. They can choose from American history, historical places, world history, and cultural history. If searchers can't find what they are looking for, browse the links to top-rated history resources for more data.

Nobel Channel

http://www.nobelchannel.com

This is a beautifully produced site with access to the largest archive of Nobel materials in the world. The Nobel Channel features rich interactive experiences with Nobel laureates and their achievements. The Interactive Learning Studio has a lesson with Eli Weisel, Holocaust survivor, writer and Nobel Peace Prize winner.

Time 100

http://cgi.pathfinder.com/time/time100/index.html

Time Magazine features the most important people of the twentieth century, as selected by its editors. Features include an overview of the major events of the twentieth century, a look ahead, and, of course the top 100—complete with biographies, timelines, images, and even sound and video clips of their work. This will be a good source of information for term papers for at least the next several years.

United States Holocaust Memorial Museum

http://www.ushmm.org/

One of the best Holocaust memorials on the Internet, this museum is extraordinarily well done in terms of content and organization. Students can learn about the Holocaust, the museum's exhibits and its functions, the work of the museum's task forces, ongoing research on the Holocaust, and current news associated with Holocaust studies. There is also a search engine to locate specific information and facts on the Holocaust.

Women in World History Curriculum

http://www.womeninworldhistory.com/

This website offers information about women in world history and quotes from some of those women. Also includes a group of seven women's history lessons, dating from ancient times to today. Ten biographies of remarkable women of history are included.

Hobbies

A hobby is hard work you wouldn't do for a living.
– Source Unknown

A-Z Collectible Classifieds

http://www.collectibleclassifieds.com/

This site provides a long list of collectibles for sale as well as news on up-coming shows, and contact details for dealers.

CODEXX!

http://www.codexx.com/

If students are true believers, then they'll love this site. It offers an exceptional collection of links to the Internet's best sites for science fiction, comic books, fantasy, gaming, sports, and movies. Everything from NASA to the X-Men can be found here. Sponsored by Edgenet Inc.

Die Cast Digest

http://www.diecastdigest.com/

For teens who are dedicated racing car collectors (or Hotwheels and diecast cars), this site will provide subscription details and sample articles from this magazine. They can also check out the chat room.

RC Online.com

http://www.rconline.com/

Packed with chat, forums, a swap shop, live cams, humor, and R-C games, as well as columns, events, a photo gallery, movie clips, and reviews. Ideal for the teen enthusiast!

Roller Coaster Database

http://www.rcdb.com/

Roller Coaster Database contains statistics on more than 600 roller coasters, which is a nearly complete list of all operating roller coasters in North America.

Sci-Finds Collectibles

http://world.std.com/~scifinds

If your teenager is into Thunderbirds, Star Wars, Star Trek, Alien, and Spawn, they'll love this site. The site also features information on how to order series figures, cards and other stuff online.

WorldWide Collectors Digest

http://www.wwcd.com/index.html

The Collectors Digest features price guides, a schedule of live auctions, club membership, and links to memorabilia dealers arranged by type of collectible.

Hobbies--Coin Collecting

Money is something you got to make in case you don't die. – Max Asnas

American Numismatic Association

http://www.money.org/

Teen coin enthusiasts will find comprehensive information on coin collecting and numerous links, with a marketplace directory and a convention schedule.

BullionCoin.com

http://www.bullioncoin.com/index.cfm

For the serious coin collector, this site features a search engine for listings of coin and bullion dealers worldwide, and related links.

CoinLink Numismatic Directory

http://www.coinlink.com

As the title indicates, this site features a large directory of sites dedicated to coin collecting including classifieds, clubs, and other helpful resources.

CoinSite

http://www.coinsite.com/

Hobbyists who enter this comprehensive website will find that it is dedicated to all things numismatic, including a trading room, tips for collectors, links, and a search engine.

Collectors.com

http://auctions.coin-universe.com/

Advanced collectors have the opportunity to bid for coins and currency online. The site offers a wide range of items for auction, which will allow viewers an opportunity to learn of trends and evolving values.

E Pluribus Unum

http://epu.mcaver.com/

This is another large database of numismatic sites. Teens may also be interested in the many well written articles on coin and currency collecting.

Gallery of World Coins

http://webpunkt.com/piotr/coins/index.html

Young people who have specialized in collecting of ancient and contemporary coins from around the globe will find that this is an invaluable guide. It is frequently updated often, and it offers many links to related sites.

Numismatists Online

http://www.numismatists.com/Q.Id3aed/

For young collectors who would like to learn more about auctions, this site offers live auctions, a directory of dealers, and instructions on how to join an auction. Includes articles on coin and currency collecting.

Hobbies--Comics

Sacred cows make the best hamburger. – Abbie Hoffman

Comic Art & Graffix Gallery Virtual Museum & Encyclopedia

http://www.comic-art.com/

A comic collector's dream come true. Comic lovers can browse through histories and biographies of artists, writers, creators, publishers, and find information on just about anyone who made a difference in the world of comics. Tour the gallery of comic art and comic book covers/stories, and a store that specializes in comic book memorabilia.

Comic Book Resources

http://www.comicbookresources.com/

As powerful and stylish as the superheroes it publicizes, this comic book site offers the latest news and gossip in the comic world. Links to favorite books on the Web, a chat room, contests, polls, are a few pleasant surprises. Sponsored by Boiling Point Productions.

ComicCompany.com

http://www.comiccompany.com/

Atlanta's largest comic book store comes to the Internet in a big way. Teens can view new and rare comic books and ccg card games, get the latest comic news, defend their favorite superhero in a chat room, and subscribe to one of the biggest comic book subscription services. Sponsored by The Comic Company.

The Comics Hotlist (Sarjakuvasivu)

http://www.uta.fi/yhteydet/sarjikset.html

From *Doonesbury* to *Dilbert*, this site offers links to virtually every comic available on the Web. Students can use this site to select their favorites and group them together on their very own personalized comic page.

Hobbies--Stamp Collecting

Patience in the present, faith in the future, and joy in the doing. – George Perera

Banknotes.com

http://www.banknotes.com/

Extensive library of images of banknotes, stamps, coins and tokens from all over the world. Collecting information is included.

Philately.com

http://www.philately.com/philately/index.htm

Teens will find convenient indexes at this site that will permit them to locate information on stamps by country and theme, as well as contacts and links to philatelic organizations and events.

Stamp Collectors Organizations

http://www.stampshows.com/clubs.html

Serious collectors will find a list of the world's stamp collecting organizations at this site—from the Aerogramme Society to the Welsh Philatelic Society. Sponsored by the Stamp Yellow Pages.

Holidays

Christmas comes. But once a year is enough.
– Anonymous

AprilFools.com

http://www.aprilfools.com/

Teens who enjoy practical jokes will have a field day with this site. They can baffle friends by sending realistic fake "notices" in the mail, like a notice recalling a new computer. They can also confound family and friends with postcards from unusual vacation spots or

put their friend in the middle of headline news with just a few clicks.

Christmas Central

http://www.rats2u.com/christmas/christmas_index.htm

Wonderful directory of sites of Christmas animations, clip art, crafts, virtual cards, Christmas music, holiday recipes, and events.

Christmas in CyberSpace

http://www.njwebworks.net/christmas/

You won't find anything about Santa Claus or the seven reindeer at this location. It is a directory of religious-related Christmas and Advent sites.

Holidays on the Net

http://www.holidays.net/

For anyone into all-out celebration, this site features a wealth of animations, music, stories, movies, games, and coloring pictures. Have students send a holiday e-mail greeting card, or encourage them to make a craft project using the directions and links contained in this source.

Kwanzaa Information Center

http://www.melanet.com/kwanzaa/

Curious to know more about Kwanzaa? All your questions are answers here. It provides concise historical and cultural background, and describes the meaning of this African American holiday. Additional information is provided on the spiritual elements of the holiday.

Mayday on the Web

http://www.accessweb.com/mayday/

Students can obtain quick information on the history of the May Day observance at this site, as well as an event calendar, an art gallery, and a summary of how May Day is celebrated around the world. Added links to related sites are an added feature.

Multi-Cultural Calendar

http://www.kidlink.org/KIDPROJ/MCC/

The Kidlink Project database contains unique ways kids from around the globe celebrate their holidays.Get recipes for holiday foods, historical background, and the cultural or religious significance of the holidays.

World Book Online: Holidays Around the World

http://www.worldbook.com/fun/holidays/html/holidays.htm

A World Book look at all of the important American holidays. The Fun & Learning section has articles that are tied to the school year curriculum, so teachers and students can take advantage of the ideas.

The Worldwide Holiday & Festival Site

http://www.holidayfestival.com

Sponsored by Hallmark, this site is a valuable collection of the national holidays of countries all over the world. It also includes an alphabetical list of religions and their related holidays. Under countries, there is information on public holidays, festivals and fiestas for each country. Religions include information on the feast and fast days observed by most major religions.

Homework Help (*See also* the specific subjects)

The more we study the more we discover our ignorance.
– Percy Bysshe Shelley

Ask an Expert

http://www.askanexpert.com/

Parents will especially appreciate this site when even they don't know the answer to an especially perplexing question. Ask an expert! Perfect for students who are assigned research projects, (and for teachers who are seeking creative ideas on how to create a student project), this site lets teens choose from twelve categories and hundreds of websites and e-mail addresses to find an expert to answer any question—from Amish lifestyle to zoo keeping. Sponsored by Pitsco, Inc.

B.J. Pinchbeck's Homework Helper

http://school.discovery.com/students/homeworkhelp/bjpinchbeck

This resource offers hundreds and hundreds of useful reference websites to help students complete their homework. Organized by subject categories such as science, music, Spanish, and current events, the categories are rated for their usefulness. Each link includes a mini-review. This site would also be helpful to teachers who are seeking resources for student assignments. Sponsored by Bruce P. Pinchbeck and B.J. Pinchbeck.

Homework Heaven

http://www.homeworkheaven.com/

If the homework answers are out there, then they can be found here, at the home of one of the biggest study sites on the Internet. Students click on an appropriate grade level to view subject categories—from algebra to foreign languages to zoology. The site has over 100 experts on hand to answer student e-mail questions.

i love teaching.com

http://www.iloveteaching.com/index.htm

The name says it all: I Love Teaching is a teacher's homepage that provides resources to help every instructor feel that way, with resources for education majors, tips for teaching job interviews, and sections for English, Science, Shakespeare and Internet classroom curriculums. This site is a member of the Classroom Connection and Teachers Resource webrings.

KidsConnect

http://www.ala.org/ICONN/AskKC.html

This is a spot for submitting that tough to answer question—answers are promised within two school days. The online question-and-answer service is operated by the American Association of School Librarians.

Lightspan.com

http://www.lightspan.com/

Lightspan links kids, teachers, and parents around the world for true global learning. The website offers teachers and students an opportunity to connect with classrooms around the world and collaborate with individuals, schools, businesses, and community organizations to design, develop, and manage hundreds of collaborative learning projects each year. Sponsored by TLN.

Schoolwork.Org

http://www.schoolwork.org

Library closed? Need information for your homework assignments? Teens might want to check this site, designed for students in grade seven and up. There are many subject links to aid in researching for reports and papers. It's not a replacement for a good library and professional staff, but it can avoid a disaster if the report is due tomorrow morning.

Study Web

http://www.studyweb.com/

Consider this site to be a student's best friend—around homework time, anyway. Here, students can easily search for sites to help them study and complete their homework on a variety of subjects —from science and music to agriculture. The entries include notations on grade level and downloadable images. Students can browse by subject category, or search the entire site's collection of over 100,000 links.

Virtual World Classroom

http://www.arch.columbia.edu/DDL/cad/A4535/ vir. world.class.html

The Virtual World Classroom is an experimental electronic learning environment. Through this website, information about advanced technologies can be shared. Work can be archived and published electronically. The Virtual World Classroom can be accessed 24 hours a day from any computer on the Web.

Humor

A man isn't poor if he can still laugh.
– Raymond Hitchcock

Absolute Madness!

http://welcome.to/madmail

This is site that promises to bring a smile with a large collection of wild, zany, and otherwise wacko stories intended to make anyone forget about their problems for a few minutes.

Alex's Humor File

http://www.rider.edu/users/grushow/humor.html

A generous supply of brief jokes, quips, funny lists, and light humor on all sorts of topics ranging from computers and politics to education and urban legends.

Comedy Web

http://www.comedyweb.co.uk/

Teens who are seeking some variety in their humor will enjoy this comedy zine from the United Kingdom. Comedy news, views, gossip, competitions, and comedy festivals around the world are featured.

comedy.com

http://comedy.com/

Get a daily dose of humor at this site sponsored by the United Internet Artists Corp. It is divided into comedy departments like People, Venues, Jokes, Media, Market, Spotlights, and of course the Joke of the Day, intended to keep your teen coming back for more.

Comedyzine.com

http://www.comedyzine.com/

No teenager can afford to be without a liberal supply of cool jokes and witty sayings. This directory of joke and humor sites on the Web should satisfy that requirement. It offers access to humor routines developed by individual stand-up comedians, as well as humor e-zines, magazines, events, newsgroups, and other resources.

Humor Space

http://www.humorspace.com/

This large humor archive is indexed by subject, with several special humor departments and a humor store. Teens will find something funny to say about almost everything when they access this site.

Humor.com

http://www.humor.com

While this is primarily a directory of Internet sites devoted to humor, it also offers a humor database, cartoons, weird news, comics and comedian home pages.

Joke of the Minute

http://www.chuckle.com/jokes/

It's true ... this site serves up a new joke once a minute, every minute of the day. If your teenager is easily distracted, you might want to omit it from your recommended list.

Joke Search

http://www.jokes.com/

Jokes on this site are indexed by subject and type.

Lunatic Lounge

http://www.lunaticlounge.com/stupidhumannoises/

The name certainly fits. Lunatics will feel right at home here. Stupid Human Noises is the subheading and it accurately describes what you will hear at this site. Listing any of these "stupid human noises" is just a bit too undignified for this directory so we'll skip the description and let your imagination take over.

1001 Jokes

http://www.netfit.net/jokes/index.shtml

If your teen feels the need for some droll humor, there is plenty of resource material on this site. Subscription is necessary, but membership is free. There is also a Joke Chat Room, and some games such as Black Jack and Connect Four.

Internet Basics (*See also* Computers)

Discovery consists of seeing what everybody has seen and thinking what nobody has thought.
– Albert Szent-Gyorgyi

Bess, the Internet Retriever

http://bess.net/

This Internet service provider can restrict access to sexually-explicit or adult-oriented material.

Fortune City

http://www.fortunecity.com/

Take a trip! Get away from it all. This site will take you to a virtual community comprised of personal homepages organized into themed districts. Any individual who agrees to abide by the conditions described in the website can obtain 20MB of free memory and use the space to create a personal Web page.

The Internet Help Desk

http://w3.one.net/~alward/

Whether your teen is a green newbie or a seasoned veteran of the Internet, this site will help both become "knowbies" in no time at all. Especially valuable are guides to using e-mail and browsers, and rules for proper netiquette.

Learn the Net: An Internet Guide & Tutorial

http://www.learnthenet.com/english/index.html

Students who are just getting their feet wet on the Internet will appreciate this step-by-step online tutorial that will guide them through the fundamentals of the Web such as e-mail, newsgroups, as well as advanced topics such as conferencing.

Newbie.NET

http://www.newbie.net/

This is another useful guide to the Internet aimed at beginners. The Cyberspace Cybercourse offers everything there is to know about the Internet. Students may wish to subscribe to the NewbieNewz mailing list, or e-mail in their questions for personal answers.

PlanetAll.com

http://www.planetall.com/

Amazon.com sponsors this free and very helpful site. Individuals can develop a personal and private address book and virtual calendar of appointments. The site can also be used to keep in contact with members of a specific group, such as classmates, and learn when their e-mail and snail mail addresses change. There is even the opportunity to develop an open a special chat room for a group.

Songweaver.com: On Netiquette

http://songweaver.com/netiquette.html

Every user of the Web would benefit by browsing through this glossary of network etiquette. It includes both the general guidelines as well as more advanced topics such as binary attachments, chain letters, and line spacing.

WebSitez

http://www.websitez.com/zhub.shtml

This is a site for parents, teachers and teens. Access to this website permits searches for specific domain addresses by entering part of a Web address, keywords, or company names. It can save considerable time when a complete URL is unknown.

thewebtools.com

http://www.thewebtools.com/tutorial/tutorial.htm

The WebTools Company developed this free online tutorial to take the mystery out of surfing the Web. It is a well-organized introduction to finding all types of needed information. The tutorial covers 48 topics, such as "How to use the right keywords, How to become a Power Searcher," and "Query Recommendations." It is enthusiastically suggested as a must-stop for all surfers.

Jobs (See Employment)

Libraries

A library is thought in cold storage. – Herbert Samuel

Internet Public Library

http://www.ipl.org

The Internet Public Library functions like a public library, and thanks to e-mail, you can even get assistance from a librarian. Access is free, and the available resources are significant. Teens will discover that it is user friendly if they possess basic library skills. This site will be a popular alternative when their school or local public library is unavailable.

LibrarySpot.com Libraries Online

http://www.libraryspot.com/librariesonline.htm

Students, teachers and librarians will appreciate this convenient, user-friendly virtual library resource that breaks through the information overload of the Web to offer access to valuable information about the best library and reference sites. Especially valuable is the insightful editorial commentary.

Libweb: Library WWW Servers

http://sunsite.berkeley.edu/Libweb/

Libweb currently lists over 2,700 pages from libraries in over 70 countries. Library researchers can browse through these pages using keywords, location, library type, name and other identifiers.

The New York Public Library

http://www.nypl.org/

The New York Public Library Online is a premier library website, getting high marks for depth, content, and design. Of particular interest to students and researchers is its Digital Library Collection, which is well worth browsing.

School Libraries on the Web

http://www.voicenet.com/~bertland/libs.html

This is a list of library Web pages maintained by K-12 school libraries in the United States and in countries around the world. The content of these pages is quite varied, and it reveals the marvelous creativity of school librarians around the world.

University of Exeter: Library and Related Resources

http://www.ex.ac.uk/library/wwwlibs.html

For a British perspective, check the libraries, museums, centers of research, and publishers that are available here. Additional sections include links to FAQ files, as well as Web indexes that make searching the ever-growing Web easier.

University of Virginia: Library Catalogs Around the World

http://www.lib.virginia.edu/natlcats.html

Users of this site will find a page of links to library catalogs around the world, indexed by region. While the number of links is small, many more resources are accessible through each catalog.

Literature (*See also* Books and Reading; Full-Text Resources)

Literature always anticipates life. It does not copy it, but it molds it to its purpose. – Oscar Wilde

Anthology of Middle English Literature (1350-1485)

http://www.luminarium.org/medlit/

Strikingly designed, this site is a comprehensive resource for studying the classics of Middle English literature. Features include author pages, portraits and other images, biographical information, related essays, other online resources, and an online store that permits students to purchase cited works. There are additional pages on renown medieval plays and lyrics.

The English Server

http://eserver.org

Developed and maintained in the English Dept. of Carnegie Mellon University, the English Server is a searchable index of over 20,000 literature and related resources around the world. Students can search by keyword, or browse categories on such topics as calls for academic papers, reference guides, languages and language theory, philosophical literature, and literally dozens more. Of note is the Drama Collection, which offer original short plays, long plays, dramatic criticism, and links to theater and drama-related resources, in a searchable database of dramas ancient (Aristophanes) and modern, famous (Shakespeare, Shaw and Ibsen) and the obscure. Contemporary playwrights can also submit their original work for inclusion on this site.

Indigenous People's Literature

http://www.indians.org/welker/natlit.htm

Dedicated to Native American literature, this site provides more than twenty expansive sections dedicated to the art and life of indigenous American peoples. Students can survey the work of particular artists, and the holdings of art museums, galleries and education centers. Of particular interest are the inspiring biographies of famous chiefs and leaders, prayers and quotations.

Internet Classics Archive

http://classics.mit.edu/

Drawn from the powerful MIT database, this site provides a collection of more than 400 titles from the classic "golden age" of literary philosophy, mainly ancient Greco-Roman texts, as well as selections from respected Persian and Chinese authors such as Confucius and Omar Khayyam (translated into English).

Legends

http://www.legends.dm.net/

Students visiting this site will obtain guided access to: primary source material and up-to-date scholarship, personal essays and extended reviews, historical surveys, and great stories. The site is divided into broad subject categories featuring the major legends such as Robin Hood, King Arthur, Pirates & Privateers, and other swashbuckling characters of balladry, fiction, and film. Each category contains detailed background on the legend. The site also contains excellent resource lists and links to other related websites.

Literary Resources on the Net

http://www.andromeda.rutgers.edu

Visitors to this site will find a searchable, indexed database providing links to thousands of books, authors, curricula and syllabi, journals and academic publications, and international literary organizations. Students can survey literary periods from medieval to modern, explore the history of the book and publishing, or search by keyword for information on the literary classics.

LitLinks: Literary Links on the Web

http://www.ualberta.ca/~amactavi/litlinks.htm

With crisp organization and expansive international content, this site offers links to major sites and resources on world literature. There are pages on authors from Austen through Wordsworth, archived classics, and literary journals and other publications. Researchers will also find links to resources on literary theory.

The Shakespeare Web

http://www.shakespeare.com/

Dedicated to the analysis and simple enjoyment of "The Great Bard," this site offers a verse game (in Java) which is similar to magnetic poetry, with famous Shakespeare quotes, an archive of questions and answers from students and aficionados, and a serio-comic look at "Today in Shakespeare History."

Sixteenth Century Renaissance English Literature (1485-1603)

http://www.luminarium.org/renlit/

Thirty of the greatest contributors to Renaissance literature are featured on this well-organized site. Users will find portraits and other images, biographical information, essays and articles, related Web resources, famous quotes from and about the authors, indices of and links to their work (including audio samples) and an online store.

WWW Medieval Resources

http://ebbs.english.vt.edu/medieval/medieval.ebbs.html

This compilation of resources addressing medieval culture includes links to academic discussion lists, including an explanation of how the discussion lists work and how to subscribe to them, an archive of texts from and about the period, including Chaucer and the Latin Vulgate Bible; and links to databases and libraries with medieval holdings.

Web Resources on American and English Literature

http://www.lib.uconn.edu/subjectareas/engweb.html

Sponsored and maintained by the University of Connecticut Libraries, this site provides links to thousands of western literature resources. It is organized by genre and era, from Old English and medieval literature and Renaissance and 17th century literature, through 20th century American, English, Irish and Welsh literature.

The Word: Literature, Journals, Books

http://www.speakeasy.org/~dbrick/Hot/word.html

This compilation of thousands of links is entirely structured around words. It begins with archives of dictionaries, encyclopedias, the Bible and other references guides, then proceeds through online books and retail sites, college newspapers and other publications, online journals and magazines, and poetry sites.

Mathematics

Logic is the anatomy of thought. – John Locke

Abacus: The Art of Calculating with Beads

http://www.ee.ryerson.ca:8080/~elf/abacus/

For those students who ever wondered what people used before the calculator was invented, this will be a fascinating experience. This site explains how people living in ancient times used to count with an abacus—a device constructed of wood and beads—and why it's still preferred today by the blind and some store clerks in Asia.

Dave's Math Tables

http://www.sisweb.com/math/tables.htm

This comprehensive collection of math reference tables is the perfect helping hand to any struggling math student—from multiplication to geometry and calculus. If it has an easy to follow reference table, it can be found here. The site also includes a real-time chat with a drawing white board for teaching and tutoring over the Net.

Frequently Asked Questions in Mathematics

http://www.cs.unb.ca/~alopez-o/math-faq/
    math-faq.html

This site offers a great compilation of Frequently Asked Questions of interest to everyone from the rank amateur all the way to the most advanced mathematician. Students will also find links to other math resources and projects on the Internet. Sponsored by the University of Waterloo.

Martindale's Reference Desk: Calculators On-line Center

http://www-sci.lib.uci.edu/HSG/RefCalculators.html

If teens think that a calculator is just for adding and subtracting, send them to this site! The activities demonstrate that calculators can be used in almost every aspect of life to calculate almost everything—from knitting and football to weather unit conversions. Students pick a category and click on a subject to get the calculated help they need—from virtually every calculator ever conceived. Plain fun even for those who have nothing to compute.

The Math Forum: Ask Dr. Math

http://forum.swarthmore.edu/dr.math/dr-math.html

This innovative website is like having your own math tutor on call, 24-hours a day. From square roots to polynomials, this math help service — made up of over 225 volunteer college students from around the globe — will answer any struggling student's questions, explaining the background behind the process, as well as the step-by-step process itself. It is all in an easy, helpful, and sometimes humorous manner that the textbooks just can't provide. It also includes mailing lists, Web-based discussion areas, math site lists, and an ask-an-expert service. Sponsored by the National Science Foundation.

Math Homework Help

http://www.erols.com/bram/

Students can receive a limited amount of assistance with math assignments at no cost at this site. If unlimited assistance is preferred, you can get it for a low monthly fee. Other free resources that are available include a timeline of famous mathematicians, a comprehensive dictionary of mathematical terms, practice problems, and basic help with algebra, geometry, trig, and more.

Math Share Shop

http://tqd.advanced.org/2897/

High school students can learn how to do their math assignments easier and more enjoyably with this comprehensive math reference service. This site offers a place to pool, exchange, and share ideas, approaches, and materials about math; a collection of reference sheets, memory aids, and visual organizers stuffed with the basic facts of high school math; and a page of common and funny mistakes to help students avoid them. Sponsored by Theodore Roosevelt HS and Edward R Murrow HS.

Money (See Finances)

Movies & Moviemaking

It's more fun than polo. It's like going undefeated in football. – Tommy Lee Jones *[When asked if making movies is fun.]*

American Film Institute

http://www.afionline.org/

A first-class, attention-grabbing gateway to the AFI Catalog of Feature Films. Countless entries, plus much more film-related information. Film buffs will love the sections on Awards, News & Events, Film Festival info and shopping the CyberShop.

California Movie Maps

http://www.gocalif.ca.gov/movies/

California has been home base for thousands of movies over the past few decades. This unique site describes those movie locations. By clicking on various regions throughout California, teens can see what movie or television show was filmed there. Bon Voyage for a fascinating journey!

E! Online Plus Movies

http://www.moviefinder.com/

Teens can get the latest movie news, link to movie sites, view trailers, and check on what's new on video. Students can be learn when a favorite movie will appear on television using the e-mail service. By registering their e-mail address and the name of the film, they can receive reminders of when that movie will appear on television.

eXposure: The Internet Resource for Young Film-makers

http://www.exposure.co.uk/

Teens can find serious articles on film-making at this site, pick up some filmmaking slang, ask questions, provide answers and join in the discussion.

The Film Maker's Home Pages

http://www.filmmaker.com

This site is an impressive online resource for filmmakers. Here students can exchange information helpful to the production and distribution of films and film-related projects. The site includes articles, FAQs, a dynamic database of links to other sites and film and video-related files for download. Other features include bulletin board style discussion areas, a live chat section, and the LOAFS (Library of Annotated Film Schools) and DUMPS (Directing Unsuccessful Motion Picture Shorts) archives. The Library of Annotated Film Schools (LOAFS) not only provides a comprehensive listing of film schools' websites from around the world, it also offers something that the film schools themselves do not reveal: honest, telling reviews

Film.com

http://www.film.com/Default.htm

If your teens are looking for Godzilla or Jurassic Park, they better skip this site. Here the focus is contemporary film review and discussion, film festivals announcements and field reports, and essays on film craft and filmmaking for the serious student.

Hollywood Movie Store

http://www.hollywoodnetwork.com/Moviestore/

Students can find memorabilia from their favorite TV show or movie at this site, with chat and secure online ordering.

Hollywood.com

http://www.hollywood.com/

All About Movies features a Movie Guide, a Video Guide, Movies on TV, Movie Talk, Movie Tunes, and Hollywood News. Teens who are serious students of the movie industry can check out the newest releases, learn the latest gossip, and get box office statistics on movies. They can also download movie soundtracks and listen to their favorite tunes. In Beneath The Surface, they can look at the latest in underground films. In Buzz Forums, they can chat about celebrities, behind-the-scenes information and movies.

Motion-Picture Industry: Behind-the-Scenes

http://library.advanced.org/10015/

A behind-the-scenes look at the motion picture industry is available at this site. Learn about the world of filmmaking by browsing the filmmaking reference section, read exclusive filmmakers interviews, and share their opinion on current films. In Observatory, they can see a student-produced film with complete computer-generated special effects, and go behind the scenes to see how it was all done. In Exploratory, teens can actually make their very own film online with a unique simulation, talk to other filmmakers in a virtual community, and even participate in making a feature film.

Movie Review Query Engine

http://www.mrqe.com/lookup?

Why should students have to wait for a movie review when they can have it come to them regularly with this all-inclusive review search engine. From the latest releases to that rare video gem, this site will access over 18,000 reviews to let teens know just what critics from around the world have to say about a specific film.

MovieClicks.com

http://www.movieclicks.com

If your teens have their appetite whetted by the coming attractions for a new movie, but they're not sure if it's really worth their time and money to see, this site contains links to the official websites for all the latest movies.

Moviefone.com

http://www.moviefone.com/

MovieFone has produced this site on movies where teens can search by the title, star and by the movie type. Access movie trailers, read reviews, get ratings and previews of the latest releases. By submitting their zip code, they can even find out what movies are playing in their own neighborhood.

movies.Net

http://www.movies.net/

Movie buffs will find an extensive list of links to movie-related stuff: Stars and Celebrities, The Studios, Now Playing, The Reviews, Movie Memorabilia, Film Festivals, Publications, Guilds and Associations, Production Resources, Show Biz News, Databases and Archives cover just about everything on the movies.

100 Years ... 100 Movies

http://www.AFIOnline.org/100movies

The American Film Institute chronicles, celebrates and commemorates the past 100 Years of America's most loved and most watched movies. Can you guess the top 10?

Whoopie!

http://www.whoopie.com/

This is a site for teens who are into audio and video. It also includes movie trailers, audio clips, animations, live video clips, music clips, celebrities, and comedy. Students can search by the artist, title or even the concept. They can also chat with others interested in the same stuff.

Yahoo's List of Filmmaking Links

http://dir.yahoo.com/Entertainment/Movies_and_
   Film/Filmmaking/

The sites listed in Yahoo's search engine cover every aspect of filmmaking from cinematography to directing to screenwriting to special effects to producing.

Museums--Directories

Civilization is a race between education and catastrophe. – H.G. Wells

Guides to Museums on the Internet

www.icom.org/vlmp/

Teachers, parents and students can use this convenient resource to discover which museums and galleries have mounted information on the Web. This page is a valuable reference to general guides to institutions that are accessible over the Internet. It is relatively plain in design, but outstanding in content.

TheLinks.com: Museums and Aquariums

http://www.museums.thelinks.com/

This brief page offers links to approximately a hundred museums of differing type across the United States. There are no descriptions, and there is no logical order, but it does contain a concise listing of many of the premier institutions.

Virtual Museums

http://maple.lemoyne.edu/~bucko/museum.html

This page offers students a wide variety of information and learning opportunities. In addition to providing live links to many important virtual museums throughout the world, it also offers an online directory of many historical images, a tour of several virtual museum sites under construction by college students, and several other museum databases.

Museum Stuff.com

http://museumstuff.com

This site is a gateway to over 300 museums and exhibits which offer online multimedia guided tours using text, pictures, sound and an occasional movie. Play interactive games, tour virtual exhibits, shop in museum stores and send a virtual postcard from your favorite museum.

Music

Without Elvis, none of us could have made it.
– Buddy Holly

AMG: All Music Guide

http://www.allmusic.com/

Did you know there are over 1,400 different music styles? This site offers a glossary of musical terms, and well written essays on folk, reggae, jazz and rock and roll, among many, many other styles.

Argus Music Searcher

http://www.fuzzlogic.com/argus/

Whether its a CD, vinyl, video, a tape, or just a tune heard on the radio three years ago, users of this specialized search engine can be sure to find it in this massive database of music. Searches don't even require the name of the artist or the title of the tune, since the search engine offers a variety of search options. Sponsored by Argus.

ArtRock Online

http://www.artrock.com/

This is a database with heaps of rock memorabilia accessible via the catalog search engine. It is organized into bands, artists, and genres.

The Breaking Artists Music Resource Center

http://www.breakingartists.com/links/index.html

Musician's Hook-Up, developed by Breaking Artists, is a totally free referral site for musicians, composers and artists. Artists can offer their songs on this website for agents, record company executives, promoters, and bands to hear. Visitors can also download links to players and encoders, so that they won't miss any new music. For teen musicians in search of a band, bands looking for a musician, this is the place!

CDNow

http://www.cdnow.com/

CDNow claims to be "the Internet's Largest Music Store" with over 300,000 CDs, cassettes, vinyl albums, music videos, laserdiscs, DVDs, movies, and T-shirts. Its site offers reviews, full discographies, real audio sound clips, and discounts. This is certain to be bookmarked by virtually every teenager who loves music.

Classical Is Cool

http://www.classicaliscool.com

The founding principle guiding this website is that classical music is for everyone, even teens. Visitors to this site can get the latest information on classical concerts, classical CDs and cassettes, classical radio and classical music fun. If your teen's computer doesn't have an appropriate plug-in to access music, this site will provide a downloadable free copy. Visitors to the site can click on an album cover to listen to a sample of the content, and to find out more about performers and musical selections.

The Concert Web

http://www.theconcertweb.com

Teens tune in here for extensive concert listings by nation, state and event. Click on the location and they can get a complete schedule of events. The site also offers directories of music-related information, links to bands, record labels, all styles of music, and an exhaustive encyclopedia of resources for musicians and music lovers alike.

88HipHop.com

http://www.88hiphop.com/

This is home to Hip-Hop on the Web. The sponsor is a commercial Net TV channel dedicated to accurate, comprehensive, and interactive coverage of Hip-Hop culture through Real Media shows, chats, magazines, and a daily news update—all available 24 hours a day and with as much style as teens require.

Hi Frequency

http://www.hifrequency.com/

Interested in the business side of the music industry? Want to know how to get into the field? Visit here to learn how to get a foot in the door. The site sponsor is a music marketing company that offers part-time internships. Students get to learn how to market today's hottest bands while getting that much-needed experience for a long-term career.

IUMA

http://www.iuma.com

IUMA, the Internet Underground Music Archive, offers a graphically neat music site. The website provides online links to more than 2000 artists. Music lovers can look up the bands by location, country or state. Sponsored by IUMA.

iMusic

http://imusic.com/showcase/

Current information on all types of music and popular artists can be located here. There is a music glossary, the latest music news, charts rankings, and reviews. Added features include artist biographies, sample audio tracks, and an audio store. Sponsored by iMusic.

Kaleidospace Soundspace

http://kspace.com/music

This is a good starting point to introduce music to kids that's a little left of mainstream. The website features a comprehensive list of Kspace artists, reviews, and sound clips—from adult contemporary and rock to Ambient. It includes a list of other cool independent music sites. Sponsored by Kaleidospace.

Lyrical Line Songwriting Resource

http://www.lyricalline.com/

Prospective songwriters can learn how to hone their skills at this site. It features helpful articles written by professionals, examples from today's biggest hits, and critiques of their own work from peers and professionals. Added attractions include links to songwriter organizations and professional companies, as well as a full-featured book and music store. Sponsored by Lyrical Line.

MTV Online

http://www.mtv.com/

Teenagers still want their MTV, and their official website is no different. It offers the latest in popular music news and reviews, exclusive MTV show information, videos and performance clips, sound samples, and even a music guide to what's happening in hometown America.

Mammoth Artists

http://www.mammothartists.com/music.htm

This is a unique music network that collects and promotes rarely heard and up-and-coming musicians. The site includes artists from every genre along with sample audio tracks, the opportunity to buy their CD or cassette online, and, for those students with dreams of stardom, a chance to list their own musical group. Sponsored by Mammoth Artists.

M.et.al Archives

http://www.webjammers.com/projects/bands.html

This huge music archive lists almost every unsigned, independent band and their website. Visitors can pick a genre and click on an artist to view biographies, pictures, news, and sound clips from the bands. This should be a good bet for teens who are interested in learning more about the music industry.

Monosyllabic Bands

http://ccwf.cc.utexas.edu/~meburns/UNK/band.html

Talk about a specialized website! If the band name has more than one syllable, it won't be here. Limited to monosyllabic named bands from Ack to Zapp, there are no descriptions, only links to the bands' home page. The list includes bands that are both living and dead, with a little tombstone to mark the dearly departed.

The Mudcat Café

http://www.mudcat.org

Surfers looking for the blues and folk music will enjoy this online magazine. This site features a searchable index of the Digital Tradition Folk Song Database that contains over 8,000 songs. Visitors can also talk with other folks interested in the blues. Sponsored by the Digital Tradition.

The Musician's Homepage

http://www.enteract.com/~digialex/

The Musician's Homepage features links to band resources for independent bands, major label bands, radio stations, recording and record labels. It offers good selections of companies that sell equipment, computers, effects processors, keyboards/MIDI, percussion and lots more. There is a tutorial entitled Music 101 that will give students and beginners the basics, a message board for classified ads and other questions, a musician search database by instrument and region, and a list of newsgroups.

Musicool

http://www.voicenet.com/~nickb/

Trying to find a band on the net? Then look no further. While not in any particular order, this site has compiled lots of well-known bands and musicians with at least five great links to websites that hold pictures, sounds, and everything that anyone would want to know about them.

MusicSearch

http://musicsearch.com/

This site claims to be the home of the Internet's Music-Only Search Site. It features a search engine that provides access to all musical styles by keyword, and a comprehensive list of discussion forums, and music-related images. Search and access is free.

Pollstar: The Concert Hotwire

http://www.pollstar.com

Pollstar is home to one of the Internet's largest and most comprehensive collections of concert tour listings. Students can get the inside stories on many bands and learn about their tours around the globe. Further, they can access the most reliable and accurate source of worldwide concert tour schedules, ticket sales results, music industry contact directories, and trade news. Pollstar's products and services include: Weekly Subscriptions, Music Industry Contact Directories, Tour Histories, Mailing Labels and Data on Disk. Sponsored by Pollstar, Inc.

rockhall.com

http://www.rockhall.com

Essential stop for any rock and roll fan. They can hear new inductees into the Hall of Fame, tour the exhibits, learn what's happening, participate in the chat room, and have a blast using the latest interactive, hyperactive, nearly radioactive technology. The site's database can also tell you which rock stars were born on your birthday, and you can e-mail Rockhall postcards to the ones you love.

RollingStone.com

http://www.rollingstone.com/sections/home/text/default.asp

The Rolling Stone Network has produced an outstanding site many grooves above the rest. In the Artists A-Z section, visitors will find information on a huge number of musicians. Or they can check out the magazine section for highlights of each monthly print magazine. The site is loaded with animated graphics and users can hear clips of new recordings. They can also read the latest music news, as well as accessing the photo archives.

She's Got the Beat

http://www.geocities.com/Nashville/4479/
   lafemme.html

For young women who want to pursue a career in music, this website's resources include a well-stocked bibliography of female artists and any possible music information related to women—including magazines, festivals, and organizations.

Singer/Song Writer Directory

http://singer-songwriter.com/

This is a very large website directory dedicated to singer/songwriters. Users can find links to the official home pages and fan sites of both new and well-known artists. Searches can be conducted by name, genre and region. There is a new site of the week, and current news from the music industry. Sponsored by J. Herman.

The Songwriting Education Resource

http://www.craftofsongwriting.com/

Even if kids can't carry a tune, they can now write one with this educational site devoted to the craft of songwriting. It features articles on starting and improving the songwriting craft and getting ahead in the music business, a listing of songwriting courses and instruction, and links to the best songwriting organizations, contests, and information. Sponsored by Danny Arena and Sara Light.

SonicNet Music Guide

http://www.sonicnet.com/guide/

Besides offering access to all types of music and artists through a powerful search engine, this site offers a review of their top album of the week, a list of links to the latest releases, brief biographical information about

selected artists, and a concise article about a specific aspect of the music industry.

Sony Music: Artists

http://www.music.sony.com/Music/ArtistInfo/

This is the official Sony music site, and it offers online access to information about stars such as Mariah Carey, Toto, and many other popular musicians. Teens can browse through their entire artist list, and get artist bios, news, concert information, audio samplers, and artist home pages. It should not be a surprise to learn that there is a full service music store on the site.

Suspended in Gaffa/Ecto Artists WWW Listings

http://miso.wwa.com/~vickie/artists/artists.html

This is a site devoted to women in music. The database lists almost every female singer, songwriter, musician, composer, and instrumentalist—from Tori Amos to Zap Momma—including websites dedicated to each artist. Sponsored by Vickie Mapes.

UBL.com

http://www.ubl.com/

This website features a database on all types of music, in addition to information and links for artists, radio stations, record labels, online events, concert information, magazines, musician information sites, music news, charts, and a music store.

WWW.VH1.com

http://www.vh1.com/

While it not as fresh or stylish as its sister music station and site, MTV, VH1's official website walks to the beat of its own drummer, focusing on music both in, and especially, a little left of mainstream. Visitors will also find all the latest in music news, reviews, previews, and happenings. Sponsored by MTV.

Wall of Sound: 404

http://www.wallofsound.com/artists/masterindex.html

Nothing probes music's hottest stars like this comprehensive music information site. With links to well over a hundred of today's most popular artists, music lovers can find biographies, reviews, news, photos, discographies, and even sound clips of their favorite bands. Sponsored by Starwave — home to Mr. Showbiz and ABCnews.com

Warner Brothers Records

http://www.wbr.com

Music lovers can get all the latest information about Warner's musicians at this site. In addition, they can initiate a tour search, get the latest news from the Newswire, tune into the WBR Jukebox, subscribe to the WBR E-Mail list, and purchase a line of Warner's merchandise at the site store. Sponsored by Warner Brothers Records.

Where Are They Now? Rock Artists

http://mag-nify.educ.monash.edu.au/DovetonNorth_
PS/whereare.htm

From the Doobie Brothers to Susan Vega, this site lets its visitors find out whatever happened to yesterday's popular music artists. It also includes an audio file of their hits and a link to a website dedicated to the wheres, whens, and whats of each lost group.

Worldwide Internet Music Resources

http://www.music.indiana.edu/music_resources/

Trying to find your favorite musician's website? Search this list by the artist's name. It covers individual musicians in every musical genre, as well as popular groups and ensembles. The database will also provide information on performance sites, research and study, the commercial world of music, and music journals and magazines. Sponsored by the William and Gayle Cook Music Library at the Indiana University School of Music.

Yahoo! Entertainment: Music: Artists by Genre

http://dir.yahoo.com/Entertainment/Music/Artists/
By_Genre

Yahoo has developed this database containing over 22,000 different musicians and/or bands. Visitors can search by the name of the artist or by type of music. From A Cappella to World Fusion.

Young Composers

http://www.youngcomposers.com/

This site is dedicated to up-and-coming artists from classical to rock, who are unlikely to be listed on the more popular websites. Visitors can hear their latest work or even earliest creations. It includes a discussion area to share thoughts and ideas with artists and listeners from around the world. Individuals who are 39 or younger

also have an opportunity to submit their own work for the world to hear. Sponsored by Able Minds, Inc.

Newsgroups

The only stupid question is the question you didn't ask.
– Anonymous

Folks Online: Folks Talk!

http://www.folksonline.com/bbs/

If you are just a bit uncomfortable using technology or if you are a relative newcomer to the Internet, you will find encouragement here. Visitors can share their Net experiences with others from all around the world.

MG's House of News Knowledge

http://www.duke.edu/~mg/usenet/

Students not familiar with newsgroups and mailing lists will become experts in no time with the help of this website. It is a compendium of newsgroup and Usenet information. Explanations are available on reading and posting to newsgroups, lists, and FAQs.

MIWorld Usenet FAQs

http://www.miworld.net/usenfaq.html

Students and newcomers will find this site provides an understandable introduction to Usenet, with an explanation of the various types of newsgroups and what to expect from each.

Newsgroup Index

http://ben-schumin.simplenet.com/newsindex/

This features a huge listing of newsgroups organized alphabetically. Users can click on a letter in the alphabet and a newsgroup will come up with that letter. Newgroups on just about every topic out there.

Online Clubs

A good motto is: Use friendliness but do not use your friends. – Frank Crane

Amigos

http://edweb.sdsu.edu/people/cguanipa/amigos/

This multinational website offers students, parents, teachers, and others an opportunity to share and celebrate their ethnic diversity. Sponsored by Pacific Bell.

Cheekfreak.com

http://www.cheekfreak.com/

For teenagers who feel that life is a mission impossible, Cheekfreak offers a site where teens help teens to help themselves. Once they've solved all of their problems, they can stay awhile to view and submit poetry, art, stories, and even music.

Cyberteens

http://www.cyberteens.com/ctmain.html

In Alien Assembly, students can create their own aliens using body clip art. Interested in Cloning? Click on "Conceiving a Clone." In an interactive short story, "discover the outcome of your choices when Sydney follows her cat into a mysterious, unexplored kingdom! A teen columnist writes Celebrity Interviews and Movie Reviews, and there are the most unusual contests.

E-Teen

http://www.geocities.com/Paris/3580/

Looking for a little fun? Teens between the ages of eight and sixteen are eligible to join this free club just for them. Members receive a club newsletter every two weeks, trade e-mail with friends, and are eligible for interesting contests.

Getting Real

http://www.gettingreal.com

If teens thought MTV's "The Real World" was gripping reality-based drama, wait till they see these nine teenagers try to spin their high school hopes and dreams into hard, cold reality. Read their actual diary entries, discuss it with teens across the world, and then stimulate the imagination with contests, college information, interviews with celebrity ex-teens, and message boards. Sponsored by Kidsites 3000.

HealthLinks: Cybertimes of Reginald

http://www.mcet.edu/healthlinks/reginald/

Dedicated to life-style issues, Cybertime follows Reginald as he experiences a new dilemma each week — from saving money to peer pressure and dating. It's a great way for teens to get information and new ideas on how to deal with these issues. Students can discuss them and form their own opinions, or read what a professional health educator has to say on the subject.

Teen 411 Online

http://www.geocities.com/SouthBeach/Cove/5855/

Go ahead and ask the Magic Eight Ball a question. Send a digital card. Take a teen poll. Read teen stories. Get your future from a daily horoscope. The advice line will answer your most personal and perplexing problem. The site is sponsored by Allison, who is a teen!

Teen-Scene

http://www.teen-scene.com/

While it is bit rough on the outside, it's what is inside that counts at this interactive website for teens. What's inside is the best in teen interests, including the latest music and movie charts, chat rooms, a pen pal locator, and links to teen organizations and college information.

teen.com

http://teen.com/

Pretty much everything that a teen would be interested in can be found here—for free. That includes chat rooms, pen pals, jokes, riddles, trivia, news, poetry, surveys, short stories, shopping, pearls of wisdom, word of the day, electronic greeting cards, recipes, fashion, music/movie/ book reviews, contests, and horoscopes. Whew.

TeenWorld Online

http://www.teenworld.com.my/

Welcome to this worldwide teenage Internet group run by teenagers for teenagers. TeenWorld serves as a "meeting point" for teens across the world with similar interests. It allows them to meet, interact, and work together on projects and activities. It features topical columns, advice, and services such as chats and postcards. Sponsored by TeenWorld International.

Teens-Online

http://www.teens-online.com/

For teens anxious to go online, there's no better place to start than this all-encompassing teen site. Chat with teens from around the world, post a message, read the latest entertainment news and reviews, peruse gossip from their favorite teen magazines, and link to other cool teen sites. Sponsored by Teens Online.

Outdoor Recreation

The best remedy for those who are afraid, lonely or unhappy is to go outside, somewhere where they can be quiet, alone with the heavens, nature and God.
– Anne Frank

Adventure Sports Online

http://www.adventuresports.com/

If it's an outdoor sport, this site is sure to list a resource about it! Visitors can click on their choice of paddle sports, water sports, winter sports, climbing and mountaineering, bicycling, or fishing. They can also check out recommended publications, organizations, shops, products, accommodations and womens sports.

AdventureTime Magazine

http://www.adventuretime.com/

Had your dose of adrenaline today? The latest reviews on extreme sport gear and access a whole community of adrenaline junkies. The site also offers a classified ad section for buying and selling used gear.

American Racing 'Zine

http://www.racecar.com/

This e-zine offers complete NASCAR coverage, including schedules, photographs, news, standings, results, and real-time chat.

American Snowmobiler Online

http://www.amsnow.com/

Anyone who is into snowmobiling, or is considering the sport, will enjoy this online edition of a very comprehensive magazine. It features news and upcoming events, racing, travel, a buyer's guide, classifieds, and a history of snowmobiling.

Backpacker's Magazine

http://www.bpbasecamp.com/

This website is an excellent companion to the print version of this hiking and backcountry magazine. Visitors will find a national trail guide, chat forums, news, advice, and an online store.

Bicycling Online

http://www.bicyclingmagazine.com/

The e-zine version features a bikefinder, articles on trips and bike care, advice about gear, news, tour results, and forums.

BikeNet

http://www.bikenet.com/

Features like product reviews, bike tests, tech advice, and daily news from the world of road racing can be found in this motorbike e-zine.

ClimbOnline

http://www.climbonline.com/

Serious climbers will find this website loaded with valuable information, including a database of climbs, a chat

area, news of environmental issues, a dictionary of climbing terminology, and climbing workouts.

Cool Running

http://www.coolrunning.com./

Cool Running is an informal network for marathon runners. Its website includes a bulletin board, weather information, a listing of clubs, and race updates.

ESPN.com: Extreme Sports

http://espn.go.com/extreme/index.html

While this site features extreme sports, it also provides scores for spectator sports, major league standings, and information on traditional sports stars. There are good articles and interviews, as well as headline news from the adventure sports scene. Visitors can also chat with sport legends and find features on exotic destinations.

The Equestrian Times

http://www.horsenews.com/

This is an essential site for equestrians. It offers reports on current international equestrian show news, events and results, as well as a classified section. It is updated regularly with information about show jumping, dressage and three-day events.

Fat Tire Online

http://www.mbronline.com/

Mountain bikers are the audience for this site. It is a weekly e-zine with news, trail guides, a bike store directory, gear reviews, and an event calendar. There are also feature articles on interesting locations and techniques.

Field & Stream

http://www.fieldandstream.com/

The grandfather of all sports magazines offers a lot of resources on its website. Features include excellent articles with many links to other related sites, gear reviews, hunting and fishing reports, humor, and a chat room for swapping tales about the big one that got away.

Fishing Line.Net

http://www.fishingline.net/

This angling and outdoors magazine has a rather plain design, but it offers a rich content of articles, advice, classifieds, product reviews, and chat.

Hang Gliding WWW

http://www.sky-adventures.com/hang/HGMPS
  HomePage.html

Both basic and advanced gliding information is covered at this site. Articles cover everything from how to steer and piloting requirements to towing options. A special feature is a discussion group for hand gliders or paragliders with plenty of archived information.

Hunting Net

http://www.hunting.net/

Hunters of all type of game will appreciate this impressive e-zine. Features include a database of 1,500 hunting businesses, a chat room, competitions, a trivia quiz, recipes, and columns.

KiteRing

http://www.dragenet.dk/kitering/

A large database of resources for the kite enthusiast, which includes links to kite stores, news, an online magazine with articles on kite flying, and chat sites.

MotoDirectory.com

http://www.moto-directory.com/

With over 4,000 links to motorcycle related sites, this directory is ideal for serious motorcycle racing enthusiasts. Features include a classified section, auction, race schedules, motorcycle e-zines, parts suppliers, salvage yards, lists of stolen motorcycles, book and video stores, a special section for women, chat rooms, and more.

Outdoor Explorer

http://www.outdoorexplorer.com/

Formerly I-bike, this well illustrated e-zine has expanded into a variety of outdoor activities including camping, hiking, skiing, paddling, climbing and biking. Visitors will find great articles on all these sports, gear reviews and sources, discussion forums, travel information, weather, photo galleries and online games.

Paint Ball World

http://www.PaintBallWorld.com/

This site offers links to paintball products and suppliers, organizations, players and teams. Visitors can also check related news and information, including events and user bulletins.

Riversport.com

http://www.riversport.com/

Canoers, kayakers, and rafters can use this website to locate recommended trips, safety information, instructors, guides, equipment suppliers, news, local information, weather forecasts, and club contacts. Sponsored by River Magazine.

Rollerblade.com

http://www.rollerblade.com/

This is a sharp site about rollerblading. Visitors can access the online directory to sections on how to get started, safety gear, sources for skates and gear, events, places, and associations. Sponsored by Rollerblade Inc.

The Skate.Net

http://www.webtrax.com/skate/

Skateboarders can find reviews and sources of skateboarding equipment, clothing and accessories. They can also locate a selection of skateboarding links and "other chill skate stuff."

USA Table Tennis

http://www.usatt.org/

The official rules, championship and rankings information, and the best way to fix dented ping pong balls. There are sample articles from the USATT magazine, a club directory, tournament schedules, membership information, and organizational news.

Ultimate Directory of Kayaking

http://www.cstone.net/users/winter/Kayakmain.htm

This is an attractively designed and well-organized site that features excellent bibliographies on kayaking resources, including sea kayaking, and building or buying equipment made "in the native tradition." There are also excellent links to retailers, clubs, newsletters, FAQs, and other paddling resources.

Windsurfer.com

http://www.windsurfer.com/

Almost everything you need to know about windsurfing can be found at this URL. Young people who are curious about windsurfing can find a helpful beginners' guide, and for those who are into the sport there are gear reviews, travel services, tips, and board design software.

World Flying Disc Federation

http://www.wfdf.org/

The official website for the World Flying Disc Federation. Frisbee fanatics can find links to news, official rules, events, standings, lists of organizations, and suppliers.

People

I keep my ideals, because in spite of everything I still believe people are really good at heart. – Anne Frank

CelebLink

http://www.celeblink.com

Celeblink is one of the best places for finding the fan pages of favorite actors, actress, singers, and others. Teens can find links to some of the most popular celebrities, such as Leonardo DiCaprio, Sandra Bullock, and Matt Damon. Teens will also enjoy the CelebLink Site of the Month.Sponsored by Jason Mei.

Entertainment Weekly Online

http://www.ew.com

This is a graphically slick site all about the entertainment industry. The format is like a newspaper with late breaking news and color photographs on the front page. Check out Movie Reviews, Tonight's TV, Music, Books, and What to Surf. Get a Free Trial to *Entertainment Weekly* which will be delivered to your door.

Jordan's Home on the Web

http://home.hawaii.rr.com/jordon/index.html

This is a personal home page developed by a teenage native of Hawaii. It is an excellent example of how the Web can be used to share personal experiences. Jordan identifies his favorite writing, offers access to his photographs of Hawaiian scenes and his family, recommends interesting links, and invites visitors to sign his guestbook.

Mr. ShowBiz

http://www.mrshowbiz.com/

This site features Entertainment News, Movie Releases, TV, Games, Music, and Celebrities. Teens can search the site for archived movie reviews, articles, and headlines. This is a first class site in every way. Site by Disney.

Role Models of the Web

http://www.rolemodel.net/

The mission of this site is to showcase outstanding role models for young adults. The website inspires youth to think about what they want to be, what they want to do, and how they'll contribute to society. Role models are presented from all walks of life and diverse cultures. The focus is on those who have been successful in their field, and who help others to realize their potential. Other features are a career checklist and a comprehensive set of links related to the featured individual.

Starbuzz

http://www.starbuzz.com/

Starbuzz is one of the biggest guides to movie stars online! Teens will find of links to hundreds and hundreds of stars, free contests and bulletin boards. The site is sponsored by Starbuzz and it has more information than you'll ever want to know about almost each and every star.

Teenagers Bedrooms

http://homepages.nildram.co.uk/~bnet101/

This site was developed by a college student, Julie Griffith, to meet the requirements for her degree. She sought to find out what teens are really all about by entering their one completely revealing yet dangerously forbidden place—their bedrooms. Visitors to this site can see for themselves what lurks in these most private of places, where teens have the most freedom to express themselves and their personalities.

Urban Legends Reference Pages

http://www.snopes.com/

The San Fernando Valley Folklore Society has an extensive search engine visitors can use to locate versions of many famous and not-so-famous urban legends. The site features quizzes, trivia, new legends, new versions of older stories, news groups, FAQs and a "randomizer" that offers a variety of legends and related facts. A message board enables visitors to ask questions, share favorite urban legends, or just chat with other "urban legenders."

Physical Fitness

The secret to long life is simple. Keep breathing. – Source Unknown

Ask the Fitness Experts

http://www.tyrell.net/~fitness/experts.html

Professional fitness gurus will answer questions on training, exercise and general sports health. Their professional backgrounds include aerobics, nutrition, weight training, aqua sports and slide training.

Body Break Online

http://www.bodybreak.com/index.html

Although the primary purpose of this site is to sell a range of bodybuilding products, it offers many useful features such as fat free recipes, speed training tips, recommended exercise routines, how to maximize energy through good nutrition, and a nutrition and fitness quiz.

Fitness Partner Connection

http://primusweb.com/fitnesspartner/

Health devotees can find many valuable resources at this URL. It features an online fitness library, healthy recipes, advice on weight management, selection criteria for fitness equipment, an activity calorie calculator, and FAQs on nutrition and fitness.

Fundamentals from the President's Council on Fitness and Sports

http://www.hoptechno.com/book11.htm

While this site is short on graphics and long on text, it offers important information about developing a healthy life-style, proper nutrition, exercise routines, and weight control. Teens will find this site offers a strong antidote to the confusing information about fitness and nutrition on the Web.

Health & Fitness Magazine

http://www.nauticom.net/www/bfit/

What are the medical perspectives surrounding extreme sports like inline skating, snowboarding, cycling, running, mountain climbing, and kayaking? For the answers, have teens view this e-zine.

The Internet's Fitness Resource

http://www.netsweat.com/

The IFR was developed to disseminate information on exercise and nutrition on the Net. It offers a comprehensive listing of fitness-related websites as well as the Fitness Instructor FAQ, the Fitness Plan, guest editorials, a fitness classified section and more.

Just Move

http://www.justmove.org

Sponsored by the American Heart Association, this site contains physical fitness news, forums, exercise diaries, training tips, and lots more.

Physical Fitness

http://www.bodybuilder.org/

This is an e-zine for and about serious bodybuilding. It includes a picture gallery with a lot of beefcake, contests and results, profiles of professionals, a chat room, training hints and information on steroids.

Shape Up America

http://www.shapeup.org/

Dr. C. Everett Koop, America's former Surgeon General, provides the latest information about safe weight management and physical fitness.

sportfit.com

http://www.sportfit.com/

Featured here are fitness tips and comments, articles on maintaining a healthy lifestyle, recommended training aids, plus a glossary of terms and principles. Experts at this site will reply to e-mail questions on health and exercise. "Virtual Personal Training" gives customized training regimens.

Strength Training Muscle Map

http://www.global-fitness.com/strength/s_map.html

Student can learn about the muscular structure of the human anatomy at this site. They'll find a detailed explanation of each muscle group, its exact location, functions, and the appropriate strength training exercises for that muscle.

Thrive Online

http://www.thriveonline.com/shape.html

Jam packed with a ton of useful tips, quizzes and fitness facts, Thrive Online offers articles on body image, weight loss and skin care. There is advice on selecting the most appropriate sport or exercise, how to tone the body, and useful tools such as a calorie calculator.

Total Fitness Resource

http://www.erols.com/srobbins/

Devotees of bodybuilding can click here for a photo gallery, quick time movies, pro rankings, anatomical diagrams, media reviews, bodybuilding dictionaries, a bodybuilding search engine, a bookstore, and training tips.

Politics (*See also* Government)

Everyone should have the right to say what they wish, and everyone should have the right to knock him down for saying it. – Samuel Johnson

Address Directory: Politicians of the World

http://www.trytel.com/~aberdeen/

How would you like to correspond with the leaders of almost 200 nations throughout the world? Their mailing addresses are listed here. Kings and queens, presidents, provincial governors, prime ministers, and assorted heads of state are all listed.

CNN: All Politics.com

http://cnn.com/ALLPOLITICS/

AllPolitics.com, maintained by CNN, provides extensive coverage and analysis of national and international political events. Each day it displays numerous new, investigative articles, special in-depth features, and a "Votewatch" section.

DebateUSA.com

http://www.debateusa.com/

DebateUSA.com provides a digital platform for the political give-and-take of democracy in action, hosting multimedia presentations for presidential, congressional and senate candidates. Added features include sections for national political news and state ballot initiatives.

Elections U.S.A.

http://www.geocities.com/CapitolHill/6228/

If it's even remotely connected to American politics, you'll find it at Elections USA, an enormous compilation of news, editorials and analyses, opinion polls and election results, plus links to political and major media organizations.

evote.com

http://www.evote.com/

Visitors to this website will gain further perspectives on national political issues. Regular sections examine international current events (and the politicians shaping them), the results of recent interactive polls, political cartoons, and more extensive analyses about politics.

Political Resources on the Net

http://www.agora.stm.it/politic/

Political Resources on the Net compiles links to political parties, government agencies and organizations, and political media outlets, arranged into eight world regions. The site also offers indices of resources arranged by nation, and a catch-all "international" section.

Political Developments

http://www.cyberenet.net/~lking/

Politics Online describes the origins and development of the democratic, communist and Machiavellian political models. Also features an archive of biographical information on prominent statesmen and orators who influenced these dynamics.

Politics, Politicians & Pundits

http://www.politicker.com/

Generally insightful—and frequently, scathingly partisan—Politicker.com offers news, analysis, satire and humor which examines the latest activities of the president, the Congress, and the often amusing relationship between the two. There are additional links to major network news outlets.

Politics1-- The #1 Net Guide to American Politics, Candidates ...

http://www.politics1.com/

Politics1 compiles links to every major (and some not-so-major) U.S. political Web resource, including the home pages for more than one dozen national political parties, biographies of major political figures, news, and more.

YPA —Young Politicians of America

http://www.ypa.org/

The Young Politicians of America (YPA) website offers information about the group's history, membership, support materials for young persons who want to begin their own local chapter, YPA newsbriefs and position papers on national and international topics, and more.

Quotations

When a thing has been said and said well, have no scruple. Take it and copy it. Tom Stoppard

Bartlett's Familiar Quotations, 9th ed.

http://www.cc.columbia.edu/acis/bartleby/bartlett/

This online resource is an early edition (1901) of John Bartlett's famous collection of passages, phrases, and proverbs from ancient and modern literature, so it does not include contemporary quotes. Nonetheless, it is a useful database. Users can search the site using keywords, or browse alphabetical and chronological indexes of authors.

Famous Quotations Network

http://www.famous-quotes.com

Over 15,000 quotes by famous persons can be found at this website, searchable alphabetically by author, subject, or quotation. There is also a list of recommended quotation dictionaries, biographies of the quoted persons, and a top ten list. Why not achieve immortality by submitting your own insightful words.

The Quotations Page

http://www.starlingtech.com/quotes/index.html

This page was originally developed as a humble list quotation resources on the Internet; but it has since evolved into a large-scale quotation site with many original resources. Features include the motivational quotation of the day, quotation of the week, and more.

Radio & Television

Life is not a dress rehearsal. This is it. – Lucinda Basset

Free TV Tickets

http://www.tvtix.com

Ever wonder how all those people on the talk shows, game shows, and sitcoms get into see the show being taped? They have tickets, that's how. Free TV Tickets provides you with all the information you need to know about schedules, ordering, and other valuable tips if your goal is to be a member of the audience. One word of caution: even if you have tickets in your hands, the wait to see a popular show can be three to four hours long!

The Museum of Questionable Nostalgia

http://www.dreamsandbones.com/museum/
    museum.htm

Remember the good 'ole days of classic television? These downloads of both audio and video clips of classic commercials will jog your memory. Many of these favorite TV shows still seen daily in syndication throughout the world. Take a look at a television commercial for that fabulous 36" doll Patti Playpal and watch Dick Clark introduce bands on *American Bandstand.* Sponsored by Digital Animation and Design.

Museum of Television and Radio

http://www.mtr.org/index.htm

A wealth of details about television and radio collections and special exhibits can be found on this site. Students can shop the museum shop and download clips of radio broadcasts.

Television Actress Web Directory

http://www.geocities.com/Hollywood/Lot/8198/
    actress.htm

Let's face it, teens spend a lot of time watching television. Here they can research their favorite TV leading women. Hundreds of female TV stars are listed, together with supermodel and celebrity links. Have they ever wanted to discuss a performance with an actor or actress? While this site can't guarantee they'll write back, it does offer a fabulous list of celebrity mailing and e-mail addresses. Sponsored by Zonetech in Ontario (Canada) the site has many other research categories ranging from animals to UFOs.

Television Stars

http://www.televisionstars.com/

Television junkies will consider this site as made in heaven. It focuses on today's television stars and their shows. Visitors can see pictures of their favorite stars, get the latest gossip, learn about their fan clubs, and how to write to them.

Xplore Television

http://www.xplore.com/xplore500/medium/
    television.html

If its true that the average person watches television for 40 hours a week, you will surely need to consult this guide to help you view more discriminately. Xplore Television brings you a complete listing of all of the significant television networks. Clicking on the Arts and Entertainment listing takes you directly to the A& E website which offers discussions, show listings and synopses, movie reviews, and video sales. Each click of the mouse brings you to another network's site which offers complete coverage of their network.

Yahoo! broadcast

http://www.AudioNet.com/music/

Surfers can hear free broadcast samples at this live streaming audio and video site. The menu includes top radio stations, concert schedules, artist interviews, your favorite radio stations from across the country, the top charts, a CD jukebox, the latest music videos.

Yahoo! broadcast: PoliceScanner.com

http://www.policescanner.com/

Surfers who would like to access emergency communications networks developed for fire, police, rail and air, can tap in through this unusual site. They can listen to air traffic controllers at the Dallas/Ft. Worth International Airport, the Los Angeles Policy Department, among other agencies.

Reading (See Books and Reading)

Reference (*See also* Dictionaries; Encyclopedias; Homework Help)

It makes little difference how many university courses or degrees a person may own. If he cannot use words to move an idea from one point to another, his education is incomplete.   Norman Cousins

---

• Address & Locator Directories

BigBook

http://www.bigbook.com/

No more searching for the yellow pages. Check out this online version of the telephone yellow pages. Users can enter a business name or category, plus the state, and the database will return is a listing of all matches by category. Click on the category for addresses, and click further for a map!

Bigfoot

http://www.bigfoot.com/

Users can gain access to the addresses of over a hundred million persons throughout the world at this site. Enter first and last names, and click Go to conduct a search.

BigYellow

http://www1.bigyellow.com/

Big Yellow lists over eleven million U.S. business listings, searchable by name. In addition, users can also search for personal e-mail addresses from this site.

Idealist

http://www.idealist.org/

For the teen idealist, log on to this searchable index of over 20,000 nonprofit agencies worldwide. Access is by name or subject. Each entry contains a brief description and a link to the agency's website. Young people seeking volunteer opportunities, publications, videos, or information on the work of these agencies will appreciate this resource. Sponsored by Action without Borders.

Internet Address Finder

http://www.iaf.net/

Users can locate the e-mail addresses of over six million persons at this page. Search is by name for an e-mail address, and by e-mail address for a name.

Langenberg.com Zip, City, Area Codes

http://zip.langenberg.com/

Find the Zip Code for any city in the country at this location, plus a variety of other information related to the Zip Codes, such as census data, distances between Zip Codes, adjacent Zip Codes, Post Office Locations and more.

Noble Internet Directories

http://www.experts.com/

Need an expert to speak at your next function? Consultants, speakers and other authorities throughout the world can testify at trials, undertake consulting assignments, or give presentations on specialized topics. Access by subject or keyword.

Telephone Directories on the Web

http://www.teldir.com/

Telephone Directories On the Web is one of the Internet's most original and most detailed index of online phone books, with links to Yellow Pages, White Pages, business directories, e-mail addresses and fax listings from all around the world.

United States Postal Service

http://www.usps.gov

Did you know that mail without a zip code not only takes much longer to arrive, but it holds up everyone else's mail as well? The official U.S. Postal Service website contains a complete list of tools for shipping or mailing. You can purchase stamps online, look up any zip code in the country and track your package.

WorldPages.com

http://www.worldpages.com/

This site will permit the user to find an e-mail address, phone number or website from over 60 yellow and white page directories, representing more than 35 countries.

• General Reference

Acronym and Abbreviation List

http://www.ucc.ie/info/net/acronyms/index.html

Teens can explore acronyms using the different search functions on this extensive database: Users can enter an acronym to see its expansion, or input a word from an expansion to see the appropriate acronym. Users can also submit acronyms not currently listed, or view the "failure" list of acronyms with undetermined expansions to see if they know the answer.

Afro-American Almanac

http://www.toptags.com/aama/

The Afro-American Almanac is an online presentation about the lives, roles and contributions of African Americans from the slave trade through the civil rights movement to the present. Biographies, important documents, and an excellent bibliography, are included along with learning games and some great folk tales.

American Studies Web

http://www.georgetown.edu/crossroads/asw/

American Studies includes economy and politics, race and ethnicity, gender and sexuality, literature and hypertext, philosophy and religion, art and material culture, performance and broadcasting, sociology and demography, region and environment, historical and archival resources, and current events. This site provides access to a wide selection of resources in these categories. Created by David Phillips.

Biography

http://www.biography.com/find/find.html

This biographical database contains over 25,000 famous individuals, past and present. Just enter a name to discover who they were, what they did, and, most importantly, why they did it. Teachers can also obtain classroom resources from this site. Sponsored by A&E Television Networks.

Electric Library

http://www.elibrary.com

The Electric Library provides immediate research solutions. Ask a question in plain English and launch a comprehensive search through more than 150 newspapers, hundreds of magazines, two international newswires, and thousands of other library resources.

Hotlist: Reference

http://sln.fi.edu/tfi/hotlists/reference.html

This is a simple page of about 45 information and education links that are quite useful or important, and quite easy to browse. No description is provided, but the titles are sufficient to identify the content. Sponsored by the Franklin Institute.

Librarians' Index to the Internet

http://lii.org/

A searchable, annotated subject directory of more than 5,000 Internet resources selected and evaluated by librarians for their usefulness. Designed for both librarians and non-librarians, it is a reliable, efficient guide to online reference tools.

Native American Bibliographies

http://www-library.stanford.edu/depts/ssrg/native/nativepm.html

Here is a large collection of Native American resources (books, articles, and government documents) arranged by chronological period, subject and/or geographical area.

PoliSci.com Headquarters

http://www.polisci.com/

A virtual political reference library, PoliSci.com devotes separate sections to news and information about each branch of the U.S. government, an international political calendar, biographies of the presidents, government statistics, world political leaders, and more.

refdesk.com: Reference

http://www.refdesk.com/

Look up newspaper/magazine articles, encyclopedias, maps, almanacs, dictionaries, quotations, fact books, yellow pages, net tutorials, shopping guides, downloads, search engines, and virtually every library resource except for the librarian. Sponsored by Bob Drudge.

Research-It!

http://www.iTools.com/research-it/research-it.html

Research-It! is a virtual reference desk that offers most of the important functions of a real one: dictionaries, encyclopedias, thesauruses, maps, telephone directories, biographical dictionaries and more. A search engine is available to help students find the specific information they need.

Success Link

http://www.successlink.org/

While originally geared for teachers across Missouri, Success Link can be successfully utilized by teachers from anywhere. By posting the best in innovative programs, resource libraries, and teaching ideas, teachers from across the nation can access and utilize successful, real-world tested ideas and programs to improve classroom instruction.

The Teen Page

http://snoopy.tblc.lib.fl.us/opl/teen.htm

This bare bones site is primarily a list of teen sites. Categories like Jobs, Reference, Entertainment, Museums, Teen Awareness, Teen Pages and The Wild Side give you an idea of what's available here. Compiled by the Oldsman Library.

Virtual Public Library Instructional Media Center

http://www.vpl-imc.org/

Over 1,500 carefully selected and annotated resources are available to students who use this site. Because of most of the resources are intended to contribute to curriculum goals and standards, this site will complement the homework helper websites.

Virtual Reference Desk

http://www.vrd.org/

While touting itself as just a reference desk, this site is more of a reference person—and nothing can be better than that. Here, students can get e-mail answers to their homework questions from quality online experts in the field. The site has a tremendous archive to search for previously-asked questions and answers in a snap. Sponsored by ERIC Clearinghouse and the National Library of Education.

UnCoverWeb

http://uncweb.carl.org/

UnCover is a database of current article information taken from over 18,000 multidisciplinary journals. Students will find that it is easy to use, and they can order fax copies of the articles from this database.

WWW Virtual Library

http://vlib.org/Overview.html

The Virtual Library is one of the oldest catalogs on the Web. In addition to its status as a pioneering website, it is widely recognized as being among the highest quality guides on the Web.

Research Papers (*See also* Homework Help)

A teacher is one who makes himself progressively unnecessary. – Thomas Carruthers

Constructing Your Research Paper

http://bob.ucsc.edu/library/ref/instruction/research/libres.htm

Students who need some help constructing their research paper can check here for invaluable tips, ranging from selecting a topic to finding resources and creating a bibliography.

Research Paper and the World-Wide Web

http://cw.prenhall.com/bookbind/pubbooks/rodrigues/

This online study guide for research papers features practice exercises; writing activities; bulletin board discussion areas; instant scoring and coaching; and many links for supplemental information.

Researchpaper.com

http://www.researchpaper.com/

Researchpaper.com currently contains a large collection of topics, ideas, and assistance for school-related research projects. It can help a student find the best information available, eliminate frustration, and get better grades. Heck, they can even take a study break and hang out in their chat room. Sponsored by the Infonautics Corporation.

Start Your Research Here

http://www.lib.odu.edu/research/tutorials/start/

As the title indicates, students can start their research here, where they will get structured help in finding, evaluating, and documenting sources for a research paper. The site recommends resources available both in the library and on the Internet. Sponsored by Perry Library, Old Dominion University.

Safety

The beaten path is the safest, but the traffic is terrible. – Jeff Taylor

Fugitive Watch

http://www.fugitive.com/

Fugitive Watch Productions has put together this site to publicize photographs and provide information about fugitives. Each person pictured is considered armed and dangerous. They are all fugitives from the law for violation of parole, probation or as suspects in various serious crimes like kidnapping, robbery and murder. Links to police and organizations devoted to missing children are included, together with an FAQ on the legal issues (such as teen drunken driving regulations) and crime prevention recommendations.

Keep Schools Safe

http://www.keepschoolssafe.org/

This site provides up-to-date information on successful school violence prevention programs. Get ideas to help communities work toward safer schools and devise the most appropriate response to reducing youth violence. Lots of tips on how parents can get involved, effective violence prevention strategies, and zero tolerance discipline codes that work.

The National Crime Prevention Council

http://www.ncpc.org/

The National Crime Prevention Council is a national nonprofit organization whose mission is to help America prevent crime and build safer, stronger communities. At this site visitors can explore the Online Resource Center for useful information about crime prevention, community building, comprehensive planning. There are even learning activities for youth.

Safe Teens

http://www.safeteens.com/

This educational safety site will teach every teen tips on being safe and how to use good judgment while surfing the Internet — from how to control what people know about you to how to maximize use of the computer and Internet. It includes cool links to safe sites for fun, homework, and more. Sponsored by the Online Safety Project.

Safe Within

http://www.safewithin.com/

This interactive resource covers all aspects of safety, security, and health, including safety suggestions for the home, school, work, personal safety, child safety, and even pet safety. Features include newsgroups, daily news updates, contests, a mailing list, and categorized tips.

We Prevent: Take a Bite Out of Crime

http://www.weprevent.org/

Millions of people across the U.S. have proved that through building a sense of community they can take easy precautions that can cut crime and reduce fear. This site gives you 10 Things You Can Do to Prevent Crime, 10 Things Your Community Can Do to Prevent Crime and 10 things Teenagers Can Do. Sponsored by the Allstate Foundation.

Science

However far modern science and techniques have fallen short of their inherent possibilities, they have taught mankind at least one lesson: Nothing is impossible. Lewis Mumford

---

• Earth Sciences

Einstein: Image and Impact

http://www.aip.org/history/einstein/

A website devoted to the life and work of one of the world's most illustrious scientists, Albert Einstein. Sections include the Formative Years, The Great Works, E=mc2, World Fame, Public Concerns, Quantum and Cosmos, Nuclear Age, Science and Philosophy, and An Essay: The World As I See It. The site offers access to over 100 pages of photographs, recordings and reproductions of Einstein's work. Sponsored by the American Institute of Physics

ChemTeam

http://dbhs.wvusd.k12.ca.us/ChemTeamIndex.html

High school chemistry students will benefit by taking this tutorial on a wide range of topics ranging from atomic structure and bonding to isomerism. The site also features a photo gallery and a humorous take on the science itself.

Earthquake Information: Reducing Earthquake Hazards

http://quake.wr.usgs.gov/

Bet you can't list 10 things you can do to reduce the hazards of earthquakes. Find out why they happen, and how to prepare for them. Read maps and lists of recent earthquakes, answer their additional questions with an earthquake FAQ, and access links to other related sites. Sponsored by the United States Geological Survey.

NASA

http://www.nasa.gov/

The infinite frontier comes to the infinite resource tool with NASA's official website. Here, students can learn about space and beyond from the scientists and educational staff of the National Aeronautics and Space Administration. The page includes links to every NASA center, up-to-the-minute news and information about NASA science and technology, and NASA's plans for taking America's aerospace program into the new century. At the NASA site, students are able to download the latest pictures from the Hubble Space Telescope, read about recent uses of NASA-developed technology by private industry, watch a short video of the first human landing on the Moon and view the latest microgravity science experiment aboard the international Space Station. Sponsored by NASA.

NASA: Welcome to the Planets

http://pds.jpl.nasa.gov/planets/

This site contains a collection of many of the beautiful photographs from NASA's planetary exploration program. Visitors will discover a series of seventeen images which have links to other images. There are detailed descriptions of each photo. Some of this information is very technical but there are lots of excellent images. Sponsored by the California Institute of Technology.

NASA: Virtual Trips to Black Holes and Neutron Stars

http://antwrp.gsfc.nasa.gov/htmltest/rjn_bht.html

This is a site appropriate for students from grade school to graduate school. Here, they will find information on black holes and neutron stars, and MPEG movies that will take them on virtual trips. The movies are scientifically accurate computer animations made with strict adherence to Einstein's General Theory of Relativity.

Nine Planets: A Multimedia Tour of the Solar System

http://seds.lpl.arizona.edu/nineplanets/nineplanets/

The Nine Planets is an overview of the history, mythology, and knowledge of each of the planets in our solar system. Each page has text and images. Some have sounds and movies. Most provide references to additional related information. Added special features include an express tour through the solar system and a visit to a NASA spacecraft.

Physics News Update

http://www.aip.org/physnews/update

If your teens have become bored with the traditional physics resources, get them interested again with this free physics digest, featuring physics news items that help explain and excite. The site includes an archive of important physics research topics and concepts, as well as physics success stories to offer a little inspiration. Sponsored by the American Institute of Physics.

Students for the Exploration and Development of Space (SEDS)

http://seds.lpl.arizona.edu/

Students who are interested in space exploration, space stations, aerospace, constellations, extra-terrestrial intelligence, comets, telescopes, and astronomy-related topics will feel right at home at this site. The special section on the Mars exploration is packed with images, articles, and links to sites about the exploration of this planet. Sponsored by the University of Arizona Chapter at the Lunar and Planetary Laboratory.

The Why Files

http://whyfiles.news.wisc.edu/

This fascinating and slightly humorous science site offers in-depth explorations of the science behind the latest headlines, helping to display real-world applications of discoveries that students are learning in school. Added features include an article archive, cool science images, and an online forum. Sponsored by the University of Wisconsin.

• Life Sciences

American Museum of Natural History

http://www.amnh.org/

Visiting this website is almost as much fun as visiting the museum. Students who lack the opportunity to personally visit this landmark will find this cybertour to be a remarkable alternative.

Biology4Kids

http://www.kapili.com/biology4kids/

Chock full of well-presented, easy-to-understand information on the chemistry of biology, how biology is studied, cell structures and ecology. Great graphics simply each concept and make the material truly simple to digest. Sponsored by Kapili Research Labs.

Cells Alive!

http://www.cellsalive.com/

This is a very graphic site starring animated and color-ful cells. Visitors can observe bacteria multiplying, white blood cells attacking bacteria, red blood cells, and various viruses. A fascinating look at how immune cells rush to the human body's aid when it is invaded with foreign cells. The GIF graphics and QuickTime videos download quickly. Sponsored by James A. Sullivan.

The Cow's Eye Dissection

http://www.exploratorium.edu/learning_studio/
   cow_eye/

This is one of the most popular demonstrations at the Exploratorium. For many years it has helped people satisfy their curiosity about what is inside an eye. Students have the opportunity to do a virtual dissection of a virtual cows eye. First, listen to an audio clip of instructions, then you can print or download a PDF file with step-by-step instructions. Also features a Cows Eye Primer, which is a brief interactive program that teaches about the parts of the eye.

Creation Vs. Evolution

http://library.advanced.org/29178/

Developed specifically for teens, this site attempts to present both sides of the debate from an objective viewpoint. The presentation was designed to offer opportunities for discussion and debate. Lesson plans and a quiz are available for classroom use.

Dinosauria On-Line

http://www.dinosauria.com

The definitive dinosaur directory. Read dinosaur arti-cles, listen to dinosaur discussions, essays on dinosaur issues, and research dinosaur materials. There's even dinosaur products to order if your appetite for dinosauria isn't satisfied.

Endangered Animals of the World

http://www.geocities.com/RainForest/Vines/1460/
   about.html

Most teens are aware of the large number of endan-gered animals, and this site describes some of the many endangered species around the world. The site is divided into several main sections: mammals, birds, and fish. Within each category, the species are organized by their taxonomic classification. Each entry contains a description of the animal, bird or fish, and the status of their condition.

The Heart: An Online Exploration

http://sln2.fi.edu/biosci/

Through this site, visitors can discover the complexities of the heart's development and structure. They can also follow the blood as it flows through the blood vessels, wander through the weblike body systems, learn how to have a healthy heart and how to monitor their heart's health, look back at the history of heart science, observe open heart surgery, listen to a heart murmur, find a glossary of medical terms related to the heart, and get information on how to keep their heart healthy with exercise. Sponsored by The Franklin Institute of Science and the Unisys Corporation.

Living Things

http://www.fi.edu/tfi/units/life/

The Franklin Institute Online sponsors this site about living things. It presents a simple, but interesting lesson on the circle of life. Discusses ecosystems, biomes and habitats under the neighborhood category. Under fami-lies, a lesson on classification, taxonomy, and phyloge-ny. Many scientific terms defined.

The MAD Scientist Library

http://www.madsci.org

This is the website for a laboratory that never sleeps. It provides an entire network of scientists waiting to provide answers to students' (and teachers') probing science questions. Students can browse and search thousands of questions (along with their answers), have fun with science through some Mad labs, and gain access to one of the largest libraries of science resources on the Web. Sponsored by the Washington University School of Medicine.

Monterey Bay Aquarium

http://www.mbayaq.org/

The E-Quarium is the Monterey Bay Aquarium online. Students can take a cyber tour of this famous bay, from wave-swept tidal pools to the depth of a vast submarine canyon. Special exhibits lead to the boundless oceans beyond.

The National Aquarium in Baltimore

http://www.aqua.org/

Teens (as well as parents and teachers) will enjoy this really cool website where they'll find fun information about the aquarium's animals, exhibits, and conserva-tion efforts. There are even some interactive games for kids to try out.

New England Aquarium

http://www.neaq.org/

The New England Aquarium is an outstanding institution, and its website provides a look inward to its staff, resources and ideas, and a look outward to the diversity of the water planet we all share.

Six Billion Human Beings

http://www.popexpo.net/eMain.html

Six billion people. Mindboggling, isn't it? This is a useful resource for teens and teachers who are seeking information on population growth. It provides statistics, articles, links to other sites that address population trends and the potential impact of these trends upon the quality of life. Every second the clock ticks, the world gains three entirely new people. If this rate continues, the world population will double every 40 years. Requires ShockWave. Thirty-six new people were just born as you read this paragraph!

Virtual Frog Dissection Kit

http://george.lbl.gov/ITG.hm.pg.docs/dissect/info.html

Have students log onto this award-winning virtual frog dissection site. The "Whole Frog Project" uses computer-based 3D visualizations to demonstrate the anatomy of a frog. By using high resolution MRI imaging, students will be able to interactively dissect a frog. Sponsored by the Lawrence Berkeley National Laboratory.

Science--Museums

Technology is dominated by two types of people: those who understand what they do not manage, and those who manage what they do not understand.
– Source Unknown

Exploratorium

http://www.exploratorium.edu/

This is the official online site of the Exploratorium, a museum of science, art, and human perception located in San Francisco. Here, students can virtually explore a generous sampling of their 650 exhibits, take part in science activities and projects, and browse their archived Webcasts, Web cams, sounds and images, and past exhibitions.

The Franklin Museum

http://sln.fi.edu/tfi/welcome.html

This is one of the most popular Philadelphia attractions, and its website has much to offer. Students should visit the online exhibits about the Heart, Ben Franklin, and the Universe. Added attractions include a virtual undersea adventure, and activities that will teach students about the science of weather forecasting.

Laserium

http://www.laserium.com/

Everything a student ever wanted to know about Laseriums and lasers and light is right here. The site also features a nice gallery of laser images, information on the related music that accompanies the laser shows, and a schedule of shows.

Museum of Science, Boston

http://www.mos.org/

Wow! Here is a website that will almost certainly stimulate young people to take a greater interest in science. Besides virtual tours of the major exhibits, the museum offers a pen pal program that allows students to correspond with scientists around the world, instructions for teachers and students on how to develop safe and cheap science experiments, low cost science experiments kits, newsletters, library resources, and on and on.

Museum of Science and Industry

http://www.msichicago.org/

This Chicago landmark is a great place for young people to visit, but for those who are unable to take the trip, the Museum's website offers lots of fun stuff, including virtual reality tours of a U-boat, an art deco passenger train, a coal mine, a fairy castle, and an airplane. Information on new exhibits, teacher classroom resources, and the museum newsletter.

National Air and Space Museum

http://www.nasm.edu/

The Smithsonian's National Air and Space Museum is one of the most popular museums in the world. Its website highlights current and forthcoming exhibits and lectures, along with online educational activities suitable for classroom and home use, which include "Exploring the Planets" and "How Things Fly." The site also offers an impressive list of links to other websites on aviation and space.

Ontario Science Centre

http://www.osc.on.ca/

The Ontario Science Center offers over 800 exhibits, and its website offers an excellent introduction to some of them (in both English and French). There are educational activities for young people who have access to multimedia computers, and links to sites that offer downloadable plug-ins that may be required to take full advantage of the educational programs

Smithsonian Institution

http://www.si.edu/

The Smithsonian is a "family" of special museums and galleries, and a visit to its website offers a description and links to each member of the family. Additional features include a search engine that offers access by name and subject, a summary of educational resources for teachers and students, publications and research activities.

Science Fairs

Ordinary people believe only in the possible. Extraordinary people visualize not what is probable or possible, but rather what is impossible. And by visualizing the impossible, they begin to see it as possible. –Cherie Carter-Scott

The Kid's Guide to Science Projects

http://setmms.tusd.k12.az.us/~jtindell/

From Getting Started to formulating a hypothesis or a question to be answered, this site is a terrific resource for finding that perfect science fair project. A nicely done site that is easy to navigate, anyone can quickly find a project for the science fair. Also offers a list of sites that answer scientific questions if the student gets particularly stuck on one issue and no one can help. Print out a checklist to make sure you have done a thorough job.

Science Fair Central

http://school.discovery.com/sciencefaircentral/

A thorough database of science fair material written by science fair expert, Janice Van Cleave. The Get Started section for students has project ideas, a handbook and links to additional information. The Science Fair Organizer helps teachers successfully sponsor a science fair at their school. Reviews how to set up committees, science project evaluation criteria, student handbooks, sample letters to parents, teachers checklist as well as plenty of good project ideas. Sponsored by the Discovery Channel.

The Ultimate Science Fair Resource

http://www.scifair.org/

A great resource for students looking for ideas, directions, resources, and articles on what to do for their science fair project. For teachers, there is a Science Fair Supply store that supplies display boards, trophies, ribbons, medals. For students, there are step-by-step instructions on making a great science fair project. From selecting a topic to writing the report to rehearsing the presentation. Stuck for ideas? Check out the Idea Bank which has an exchange where students can get new ideas.

The World-Wide Web Virtual Library: Science Fairs

http://physics.usc.edu/~gould/ScienceFairs/

A comprehensive list of every science fair accessible through the World Wide Web, whether of global, local or virtual in scope. A list of the most prestigious sources of contests, fairs, competitions, scholarships, tuition grants, internships, scientific field trips throughout the world.

Search Engines (*See also* Internet Basics)

Between truth and the search for it, I choose the second. – Bernard Berenson

All-in-One Search Page

http://www.allonesearch.com/

The All-in-One Search Page is a compilation of powerful search engines all on one page. One search engine allows users to find the lowest price on the Web for merchandise. The Lyrics Server can help the user find the words to a song. The Alta Vista Photo Finder can search through literally millions of pictures and images. The Lycos Pictures and Sounds engine can search through over eighteen million Web images and sounds.

AltaVista

http://www.altavista.com/

AltaVista is among the most popular search engines, and it features a Web and Usenet News searcher, indexing over 100 million pages. Primary search categories are: simple, people, business, subject, and advanced searches.

alltheweb.com

http://www.alltheweb.com/

If your teen doesn't have a clue where to find needed information, suggest this resource. Users enter words or phrases to conduct "all the Web" searches using this very fast search engine.

Deja.com

http://www.dejanews.com/

This engine offers quick or power searching of news-groups and information within newsgroups. It can help users find a newsgroup to fit virtually every interest.

Excite

http://www.excite.com/

This well-known and popular search engine can be used to search by keywords or text strings, or alternatively, it can be used to quickly browse through the various categories of reviewed sites.

Infoseek

http://www.infoseek.com:80/Home

This is another popular search engine with annotated reviews of each site. Search the Web, e-mail addresses, newsgroups or a company directory by keyword, name or full questions.

Lycos

http://www.lycos.com/

This search engine can be customized to permit users to either enter a search string or browse the Web by subject. A newcomers' section is another nice feature.

Mamma: Mother of All Search Engines

http://www.mamma.com/

This offers multi-engine searching of websites, magazines, newspapers, newsgroups, companies, and MP3 files.

MetaCrawler

http://metacrawler.com/index.html

If a surfer can't decide which search engine to use, MetaCrawler will send a keyword search query to Lycos, WebCrawler, Excite, Alta Vista, Yahoo, HotBot, and Galaxy. It will then sort the results by locality or relevance.

SavvySearch

http://www.savvysearch.com/

This is still another engine with the capability to send a query to multiple search engines on the Internet and collate the results. In addition, the user is given the choice of conducting the search in over fifteen languages.

Netstrider: Search Engines, Indexes, Directories and Libraries

http://www.netstrider.com/search/

This site not only lists, but also briefly describes the strengths and weaknesses of the major search engines. It's a great starting place to learn how to chose which of the hundreds of search engines are best for finding what you need. Visitors can also take an online tutorial, "The Search Logic Tutorial," to help them understand the artificial intelligence of a search engine so users can feed in the appropriate keywords to retrieve the right answers. Sponsored by NetStrider.

Yahoo's Listing of All-In-One Search Engines

http://dir.yahoo.com/Computers_and_Internet/
Internet/World_Wide_Web/Searching_the_Web/
All_in_One_Search_Pages/

Yahoo is one of the oldest and most used search engines, and it has compiled a huge list of general and special engines. Some of these search engines now use hundreds of different search engines to produce a complete list of what the user is seeking. Yahoo's list of sites provides names and links, but also handy descriptions of each search engine so users can choose the one that is perfect for the individual's searching requirements. Yahooligans is a search engine just for younger kids.

Shareware (See Computers-- Shareware)

Shopping

You don't have to buy from anyone. You don't have to work at any particular job. You don't have to participate in any given relationship. You can choose.
– Harry Browne

Best by Mail

http://www.BestByMail.com

This site offers a "gift selector" which allows the shopper to narrow down the product choices by occasion (e.g., birthday, holiday, wedding, etc.), type of product (e.g., jewelry, books, electronics, etc.), and type of recipient (e.g., man, woman, child, etc.). Like most reputable online merchants, this site offers a secure ordering procedure. Most major credit cards are accepted.

Brandpoint

http://www.brandpoint.com

Brandpoint offers direct links to more than 500 leading brand-name retailers, direct mail merchants, manufacturers, and service providers located in 50 countries. The main menu consists of twelve different general product categories such as toys and travel. By clicking on a specific product category, shoppers are presented with a list of links to manufacturers and merchants organized by sub-category.

Designers Direct

http://www.designersdirect.com

Designers Direct specializes in men's and women's clothing, footwear and eyewear. Besides offering special sale features, the site has a search engine that allows shoppers to search for specific products. Like many e-merchants, Designers Direct offers a "shopping cart" feature that allows shoppers to simplify selection and ordering.

Einsteins Emporium

http://www.einsteins-emporium.com

A variety of scientific and educational products can be ordered from Einstein's Emporium, which claims to be the Web's largest science and nature store. This site has over 1,000 pages of products grouped under broad subject categories such as "Living On Earth." Once a category has been selected, shoppers can narrow their search by subject and type of product. Products include books, posters, experiments, games, and more.

Online Shopping Safety

http://fullcoverage.yahoo.com/Full_Coverage/
   Business/Online_Shopping_Safety/

While everybody seems to be ordering everything online from birthday presents to car parts, it is important to remember a few important tips before sending your credit card numbers out to cyberspace and into potential bad guys hands. Yahoo's guide to shopping safely on the Internet provides the consumer with solid advice about how to ensure you are buying from a legitimate merchant, how to protect yourself from identity theft, and many other resources designed to protect the consumer from fraudulent sites.

Reel.com

http://www.reel.com

This site is the #1 online video seller—and it's easy to see why. It offers over 100,000 movies for sale and rental, in addition to helpful information on the stars, directors, and similar movies, including virtually any film ever available on video, from mainstream Hollywood to hard-to-find foreign art-house flicks. Also includes movie news and reviews on current releases. Sponsored by Reel.com

Total E

http://www.totalE.com

Specializing in music, videos and DVDs, Total E claims to stock over 150,000 albums and 35, 000 videos. Detailed information is available on the products, together with thousands of audio clips. A search engine is provided that permits shoppers to find specific videos, CDs and DVDs by title, artist, song title and key words.

Shopping--Auctions

No one ever went broke by saying no too often.
– Harvey Mackay

Internet Shopping Network (ISN)

http://www.isn.com/

Internet Shopping Network (ISN) is the home of First Auction. Membership is required in order to submit bids on products such as jewelry, housewares, electronics, and clothing. Special features include a tutorial on how to bid, short "flash" auctions which are run many times during the day, and a search engine to locate specific products. Prices start at $1.00.

eBay

http://ebay.com

eBay is the foremost online auction where you can find an unbelievable four million auctions, and 450,000 new items joining the "for sale" list every 24 hours. An unprecedented 1.5 billion pages are viewed per month. The number of unique visitors on an average daily basis sets an online record of 1.782 million. Buyers can choose from over 4,400 categories, including collectibles, antiques, sports memorabilia, computers, toys, dolls, figures, coins, stamps, books, magazines, music, pottery, glass, photography, electronics, jewelry, gemstones, and much more. Users can find the unique and the interesting on eBay. Everything from chintz china to chairs, teddy bears to trains, and furniture to figurines.

Yahoo's List of Auctions

http://dir.yahoo.com/Business_and_Economy/Companies/Auctions/Online_Auctions/

Yahoo's list of auctions is impressive in number, and all types of auctions are included (e.g., reverse auctions, flea markets, celebrity auctions, etc.). The variety of products available for bid is reminiscent of a world bazaar-wedding gowns, travel to exotic places, rare books, original art, construction equipment, business furniture, and almost everything, including kitchen sinks.

Shopping--Directories

Most of life is choices, and the rest is pure dumb luck.
– Marian Erickson

Consumer World

http://www.consumerworld.org

Consumer World® offers access to over 2,000 sites offering consumer products and services. Besides offering a product/service search engine, the site provides buying advice and product reviews, comparison shopping for bargains, aid in making last minute travel arrangements, the ability to file a consumer complaint, access to consumer rights booklets, application procedures for low rate credit cards or mortgages, wholesale car prices, personal finance tips, news of the latest consumer scams, consumer laws, and electronic coupons.

coolshopping.com

http://www.coolshopping.com/

Cool Shopping has its own online soap opera. It's design permits shoppers to keep track of the activities of the main characters while they are shopping for the best bargains. Other special features include Hot Deals and What's New to simplify navigation, shopping guides, community bulletin boards, and even shopping chat. Sponsored by the Infotique.

CouchPotato.NET

http://www.couchpotatoe.net

Couch Potato Net is a directory of stores on the Net. With an index that looks like it came straight out of a Yahoo page, this site is well organized and extensive in its offerings. Shoppers can search for specific brands, types of merchandise, gift ideas, or look for specialized online stores or catalogs.

Smoking (Substance Abuse)

Software (See Computers--Software)

Sports (*See also* Outdoor Recreation)
Do you know what my favorite part of the game is?
The opportunity to play. – Mike Singletary

AllSports

http://www.allsports.com/

AllSports is a website dedicated to one thing—sports. Coverage includes football, hockey, basketball, baseball, and soccer. Besides providing links to the major sports media sites, this website publishes reports on events prepared by fans. Each team is represented by a fan reporter to ensure that coverage is complete.

CBS SportsLine

http://cbs.sportsline.com

It would be difficult to find any aspect of sports that is not included in this comprehensive website. Features include news of world sports, women's sports, superstars, sports jobs, health & fitness, and recreational sports. If it happened, is happening, or will happen in the world of sports, visitors to this site are sure to learn all about it at this site. Sponsored by CBS.

CNN/SI

http://cnnsi.com

CNN has teamed up with *Sports Illustrated* to offer this comprehensive sports site. From baseball, pro football, college football, pro basketball, hockey, golf, tennis, soccer, motor sports, women's sports, scoreboards, it can probably be found at this URL.

ESPN SportsZone

http://espn.go.com/

The folks at ESPN have developed this excellent site that features headline sports news, sports events throughout the world, and a section called "today's best," featuring the "sport pick of the day." Special sections include Sportscentury, Training Room, and Video Game Reviews. Fans can even buy their favorite sports paraphernalia at the ESPN store.

MSNBC Sports

http://www.msnbc.com/news/SPT_Front.asp

NBC Sports and The Sporting News have jointly developed this excellent website which offers up-to-the-minute coverage of virtually every aspect of sports throughout the world. Sharply focused articles report the latest analysis on who's got the best chance of winning against whom.

USA Today Sports

http://www.usatoday.com/sports/sfront.htm

USA Today covers every sport from the NBA, NFL, NHL, to college sports to tennis, horseracing and the Olympics. Their site includes special features like Game Matchups, Ratings, Transactions, Vegas Odds, Columnists, Lotteries, Ski Reports, Sports Index, Owners Box, and Wall Street Sports.

Study Abroad (See also Travel)

The time to enjoy a European tour is about three weeks after you unpack. – George Ade

Brain Track

http://www.braintrack.com/

Know teens looking for the perfect school in Zaire? With over 4,750 links to higher educational institutions in 144 countries, Braintrack will link students to the school they want, in the region they want —all around the world. This site includes a large index of universities, polytechnics, colleges, and more.

Collegiate Choice Walking Tours

http://www.collegiatechoice.com/

Let your teens visit the colleges and universities that are of interest to them through these simple, non-promotional videos. Parents can save time and money by ordering videotaped guided campus tours from this site. Tapes are available for over 300 colleges and universities in the U.S., Canada, England, Ireland, and Scotland.

National Registration Center for Study Abroad

http://www.nrcsa.com/

NRCSA is a national consortium of over 125 organizations that sponsor programs for students to study abroad. Whether the student would like to a study in a foreign country for a few days or a few months or even

years, this resource will offer a wide selection of programs. NRCSA works with schools in 30 countries, maintains current information about their programs, fees, schedules, criteria, and lodging options. Over 15,000 students have participated in these programs. Use their simplified search engine to find a program suited to your needs.

Study Abroad Links

http://www.studyabroadlinks.com/

Study Abroad Links is an excellent resource for starting the search for a program to study abroad. Divided into categories like Summer Programs, Academic year and Semester Programs, Art Schools and Programs, Homestay Programs. Internships and Experiential Programs, Programs for High school Students, and Sports and Outdoor Learning Programs. Subscribe to their free e-mail newsletter for staying up-to-date on notable study abroad programs.

Substance Abuse

There are no rewards or punishments — only consequences. – Dean William R. Inge

• Drugs & Alcohol

Alateen

http://www.al-anon.org/alateen.html

Alateen is for young people whose lives have been affected by someone else's drinking. At this website young people learn about the organization, find meeting locations, gain advice on how to cope with an alcoholic friend or family member, and gain access to other helpful resources. Most important of all, however, is the chance to meet other teens facing similar problems.

Arf

http://www.arf.org/

Besides presenting drug-treatment options, the Addiction Research Foundation offers extensive information on the effects, composition, signs, and devastating results of almost every drug available to high school students today. Comprehensive statistics on the extent of drug abuse can also be found at this site. Information is available in both English and French.

Driving Under the Influence

http://library.advanced.org/23713/frameset.html

This site is dedicated to the dissemination of potentially life-saving information about driving under the influence of alcohol and other drugs. The introduction is divided into four parts:The Problem, The Drugs, The Effects, and Your Turn. Visitors will learn about drunk and drugged driving, why it is a life-threatening issue, and what can be done to help stop it. One other feature of the site, Getting Personal, is a multimedia supplement to the material in the introduction. Viewers will see interviews with people who have had frightening first-hand experiences with drunk driving.

MADD Online

http://www.madd.org/

Mothers Against Drunk Driving (MADD) is "more than just a bunch of angry moms. We're real people, moms, dads, young people, and other individuals just trying to make a difference. We are determined to stop drunk driving and to support victims of this violent crime." Information on membership, local chapters, free e-mail, statistics, links to related organizations, and news can all be found at this official site.

Marijuana: Facts for Teens

http://www.nida.nih.gov/MarijBroch/Marijteens.html

The National Institute on Drug Abuse has developed this simple, yet effective site that answers seventeen important questions on the use of marijuana. Do you know how many teens really smoke marijuana? Do you know what happens to your brain when you smoke it? Is it addictive? What are the long term effects? For answers to these and many other questions, tune in to this site.

• Smoking

ASH's Teen Page

http://ash.org/teens.html

Essentially, this is a list of links for teens seeking accurate information on the dangers of smoking. Sponsored by ASH, a 30-year-old national legal-action antismoking organization, this site literally contains everything for everybody concerned about teen smoking and protecting the rights of nonsmokers, including the facts on teen smoking and how to discourage it.

Smoking from All Sides

http://www.cs.brown.edu/~lsh/docs/health.html

Students will find this is a useful one stop site for everything they need to know about how smoking

affects their health. It describes in vivid detail the dangers to the lungs and the effects on the brain. This site also will links teens to the latest articles and reports on the health aspects of smoking.

Smoking Handbook

http://www.westnet.com/~rickd/smoke/smoke1.html

Since most smokers develop their habit in the teen years, this site decided to target middle school students with information about the hazards of smoking. The result is a light, yet hard-hitting guide to what tobacco and nicotine are, the reasons why people start smoking, and the particular allure of smoking for teenagers. It also includes links to other Web resources. Sponsored by the Eastchester Middle School.

Web Pages United Against Smoking

http://wilstar.net/nosmoke.htm

This grassroots anti-smoking site offers teens the chance to make their own personal website a "non-smoking site" by displaying a non-smoking symbol and spreading the word against smoking. It also contains useful links to sites with smoking statistics, helpful methods to stop smoking, as well as graphics to paste on personal sites.

Suicide (See Crisis Intervention)

Teen Pregnancy

Young people need models, not critics. – John Wooden

Abortion Alternatives

http://www.abortionalternatives.com/

This is a site for pregnant teens who want to be informed about alternatives to abortion. This site provides honest, straightforward information on adoption, single parenting, places to seek help and counseling, and all the facts and statistics that could effect a pregnant teen's life.

Campaign for Our Children

http://www.cfoc.org/

The Campaign for Our Children is a nonprofit organization whose mission is to organize, manage and conduct programs designed to reduce the incidence of teenage pregnancies. Teens can find information at this site about the CFOC, recent news articles on teen pregnancy, and resources that promote sexual abstinence. The site also offers resources for teachers and parents. Among the added features of the site is a teen pregnancy clock.

Closer Look at Teen Pregnancy

http://www.intac.com/~jdeck/tahra/Tp1.html

This site offers a close-up look at teen pregnancy through the experience of several teenage mothers. With words and photos, visitors to the site learn about the changes that had to take place after the teens became pregnant. Other features include a profile of pregnant teens and a description of successful programs.

Not Me, Not Now

http://www.notmenotnow.org/

Taking a proactive approach to teen pregnancy, Not Me, Not Now spreads the simple message of abstinence in a practical manner that is neither preachy nor dull. Added features include a guide on talking to kids and students about sex, and an interactive section for teens to learn the facts about sex and peer pressure. Sponsored by Monroe County, New York.

Prevention Teen Pregnancy

http://www.teenpregnancy.org/

More of a resource for parents than teens, this well designed site is packed with information to help prevent teen pregnancy. Included are the latest facts and statistics on teen pregnancy, a discussion forum, links to related sites, and tips for parents. Sponsored by the National Campaign to Prevent Teen Pregnancy.

Teen Pregnancy

http://web.bu.edu/COHIS/teenpreg/teenpreg.htm

Visitors to this website will find an in-depth, comprehensive resource on every aspect of teen pregnancy—from stages of pregnancy and postnatal care to where teenage mothers can go for help. If students have a question about teen pregnancy, this site has the answer. Sponsored by Boston University's Community Outreach Health Information System.

Teen Pregnancy: Facts You Should Know

http://www.noah.cuny.edu/pregnancy/march_of_
    dimes/pre_preg.plan/teenfact.html

In addition to the facts about teen pregnancy, this site provides valuable information regarding health risks to teenage mothers, health risks to the baby, consequences of teenage pregnancy, information about the March of Dimes Birth Defects Foundation, and a list of resources and links to related programs. The March of Dimes

sponsors this site to further its mission "to improve the health of babies by preventing birth defects and infant mortality."

Theatre

It's one of the tragic ironies of the theatre that the only one in it who can count on steady work is the night watchman. –Tallulah Bankhead

Theatricopia

http://www.saintmarys.edu/~jhobgood/Jill/theatre.
html

This site features a compilation of general theater and musical sites. Information is organized by categories for awards, books, composers, games, general sites, lyrics, magazines, mailing lists, multimedia, performers, shows, and shops. Sponsored by Jill Hobgood.

Welcome to the Dramatic Exchange

http://www.dramex.org/

Prospective playwrights can use this website to promote their work. New plays can be posted here, where they can be "discovered" by agents and publishers. There is an FAQ on the site and its mission, a calendar of festivals and other theatrical events, and of course, links to related sites. The plays include titles, authors, synopses and how to contact the playwrights. Sponsored by Rob Knop and Mike Dederian.

Travel

If you look like your passport picture, you're too ill to travel. – Will Kommen

Backpackers International Hostels

http://www.backpackers.com.au/bpworld.htm

Looking for true adventure? This site offers information on backpacker hostels across the world, as well as links to individual Web pages where available.

MapQuest

http://www.mapquest.com/

Never get lost again! This handy site asks only for the address of your departure point and your destination. With a click, a detailed description of the route, together with a map will be generated. The site is primarily for North American travel. Additional features include the ability to zoom in and out on the locations, and the ability to generate detailed maps of major cities.

Travel.com

http://www.travel.com/

Whatever method of travel is preferred, this site can be used to make the reservations and plan the trip. Air, rail, cruises, bus tickets, and lodging can be purchased. Additional features include currency exchange rates, and sources for travel equipment.

Travel.org

http://travel.org/index.html

This site is organized for the world traveler. Clicking on a preferred continent or nation will allow the user to reserve transportation and lodging for that region, and link with a large variety of travel agents, tour guides, and other traveler's resources. A free e-mail service will notify recipients of special tours and travel bargains. Sponsored by TravelScope.

TravelWeb

http://www.travelweb.com/

Travelers can learn which hotels are available at locations throughout the world, compare rates, and determine whether rooms can be booked. Reservations for most major airlines can also be scheduled on this same website. Other features include travel resources, bargain fares, a travelzine, and weekend specials.

Virtual Cards

Never fear shadows. They simply mean there's a light nearby. – Ruth Renkei

Best Flowers

http://www.bestflowers.com/postcards/index.cfm

Flowers are only one of many greetings that can be sent from this site. Other options include waterfalls, scenery, Garfield cartoons, and more. Select a category, and a design, add music if you wish, and then type the address of the recipient. The postcard will go out in an instant.

Cyber-Cards.com: Electronic Greeting Cards

http://www.cyber-cards.com/

This is another site similar to the previous entry, but it offers a wider range of designs. Images can include birds, butterflies, cats, dogs, horses, and wildlife. A

scenery selection has deserts, landmarks, landscapes, scenic wonders, and outer space. The "unique" category has angels, cyberspace, family album, graffiti, horoscope, office humor, and personal poetry.

E-Bouquet

http://www.800send.com/eflower/sendflower.html

This virtual flower shop sends an electronic bouquet from a selection of arrangements to anyone you wish. Their system will notify the recipient via e-mail with instructions on how to get the electronic bouquet from their server via the world wide web.

1001 Postcards

http://www.postcards.org/

Digital postcards are the latest rage, and this is the perfect source. Users have a choice of 1001 of the animated, photographic, cartoon, holiday, classic, and illustrated postcards. Every holiday is here, plus the usual anniversary, birthday and sympathy message cards, as well as a variety of unusual and fun greetings.

Virtual Trips

The best thing about the future is that it comes only one day at a time. – Abraham Lincoln

The Bosnian Virtual Fieldtrip

http://geog.gmu.edu/gess/jwc/bosnia/bosnia.html

The history of Bosnia and the actions which led to this war are covered in this virtual field trip. In addition, this site offers thoughtful discussion questions on the war and U.S. involvement in the conflict. There are also current news reports on developments affecting this part of the world. Sponsored by George Mason University.

CARE

http://www.care.org/virtual_trip/mali/

A beautifully designed site that takes you on a virtual trip with CARE, the humanitarian relief agency, to Mali. Great photographs make this a memorable journey. Read the journal entries from CARE workers who are providing famine and drought relief to the people of Mali. Learn about the work of CARE and the many ways in which they seek to impact the lives of people throughout the world.

Field Trip to Washington, DC

http://www.peotone.will.k12.il.us/fs/examples/ trip.html

Take this virtual field trip and see all the famous sights around the nations capitol. All of the important memorials are included from the Vietnam Memorial to the Lincoln Memorial and the Holocaust Memorial Museum. Stroll through the National Mall and stop in at any one of the Smithsonian Museums.

The Virtual Field Trips Site

http://www.field-guides.com/

Take virtual trips to deserts, salt marshes, tornadoes, volcanoes, hurricanes, oceans, natural wonders of the world. In this interactive website, you will see photographs, quizzes, fact sheets, and even scenic departures from the main trip. A virtual trip about volcanoes took us on a side trip to the islands of Hawaii. Also available at this site is Tourmaker, software that enables anyone to create their own Web tours.

Voluntarism (*See also* Activism)

Be the change you want to see in this world.
– Mahatma Ghandi

The American Institute for Public Service

http://www.aips.org/

Looking to inspire and reward students for community service? How does recognition by the President of the United States sound? This government organization is dedicated to attracting young Americans into community and public service by recognizing their volunteer efforts with pins and certificates signed by the President himself. You can even submit a nomination for a classmate.

American Society of Directors of Volunteer Services

http://www.asdvs.org/

Are your teens interested in volunteering at a local hospital? Then start here, with some invaluable help from the leader in healthcare volunteer services and the only national professional organization for directors of volunteer services in healthcare. Includes access to the world's largest collection of hospital literature with over 300 publications and audiovisual resources. Sponsored by ADVS.

Do Something

http://www.dosomething.org/

This national, nonprofit organization provides training, inspiration, guidance, and financial resources for our youth under 30 who want to make a difference and do something in their community. It is full of terrific projects, challenges, grants, and awards that prove teens can change the world by themselves.

Hearts and Minds

http://www.heartsandminds.org/

Looking to do some community service, but having a hard time finding the right project? Send teens to this nonprofit organization that successfully motivates people to get involved, connecting them with sources in need of help-from poverty and racism to the environment—making their volunteering efforts more fulfilling and effective. Sponsored by Hearts and Minds.

Independent Sector

http://www.indepsec.org/

This national leadership forum is dedicated to encouraging philanthropy, volunteering, not-for-profit initiatives, and citizen action to better serve people and communities. It offers numerous programs and publications featuring information on fundraising, volunteer services, and philanthropy. Sponsored by the Independent Sector.

Jumpstart

http://www.jstart.org/

Jumpstart is a nonprofit organization that engages young people in service to their community. Jumpstart partners with local early childhood providers to use the power of community service to build school success, family involvement, and future teachers, one child at a time. Find out what you can do right here. Sponsored by Jumpstart.

A Legal Handbook for Nonprofit Corporation Volunteers

http://www.ptialaska.net/~jdewitt/vlh/

Is your teen studying nonprofit corporations in class? Is she or he thinking of volunteering the for a volunteer project? Then you need this in-depth legal handbook that will guide and direct you through every legal aspect a volunteer may encounter—from creating nonprofit corporations to restrictions and uses of funds. Sponsored by Guess & Rudd P.C

Neighborhoods Online

http://www.libertynet.org/nol/natl.html

The one community service site that affects teens where they live. This online resource center directs people in building strong safe communities by providing fast access to information and ideas covering all aspects of neighborhood revitalization and creating a national network of activists. Sponsored by the Institute for the Study of Civic Values and Philadelphia's LibertyNet.

Volunteer Match

http://www.volunteermatch.org/

Looking for that walk-a-thon, beach day clean up, meal delivery, or other volunteer service in your community? Let Volunteer Match find the perfect volunteer opportunity. Contains thousands of one-time and ongoing opportunities by zip code, category, and date. Sponsored by Impact Online Incorporated.

Youth Resources

http://www.youthresources.org/

Since its inception, Youth Resources of Southwestern Indiana has engaged over 28,000 youth in 422 community service projects. In other words, this is the perfect place to get your class involved in the community and get your community involved with the youth and the issues they face.

Website Design

Reason can answer questions, but imagination has to ask them. – Ralph Gerard

Beginner's Guide to HTML

http://www.ncsa.uiuc.edu/General/Internet/WWW/
   HTMLPrimer.html

The National Center for Supercomputing Applications at the University of Illinois has designed a tutorial to teach HTML to beginners. It starts off with a list of FAQs and takes students step-by-step into the world of HTML code. HTML is Hypertext Markup Language, the language used to make Web pages. This is one of the first, and still one of the best resources for beginners, as well as more advanced users.

Creating a Successful Web Page

http://www.hooked.net/~larrylin/web.htm

This page offers an extensively cross-referenced guide for beginners and experts alike. It includes topics others usually miss, such as how to decide on content.

Great Website Design Tips

http://www.unplug.com/great/

The name of the site pretty much says it all. Visitors will find tips for beginners, advanced users, and experts. The good news is an individual can go from beginner to expert quickly. Added features include graphic design ideas, backgrounds, fonts, pictures, and animations to reflect individual styles.

A Guide to Creating a Successful Web Site

http://www.hooked.net/~larrylin/web.htm

Anyone who would like advice on creating a personal website will find expert help here. The site offers ideas on what content to include, how to organize and add style, and other useful tricks and tips. A section on how to create HTML documents will help even the rank amateur get started.

HTML Quick Reference

http://www.cc.ukans.edu/~acs/docs/other/shtml

For individuals who are seeking the details of how to start using HTML and what the language looks like, this is the place! There are lots of interesting examples and easy-to-understand explanations.

Idiot's Guide to Making a Homepage

http://www.voyager.co.nz/~bsimpson/html.htm

Designed specifically for the amateur, the total novice, and the no-nothing beginner, this easy-to-follow step-by-step guide can teach virtually everyone how to create their own website.

Net Tips for Writers and Designers

http://www.dsiegel.com/tips/

This site was developed by an expert designer to help individuals create their own personal home pages. Many excellent examples of good, mediocre and horrible page design are given. Emphasis is on type design, layout methods, using images, and selling in cyberspace.

Weave Your Web

http://www.msg.net/tutorial/

This website features a step-by-step tutorial on "How to Create Your Own Web Page." It takes the novice from the very beginning through an advanced approach. The tutorial also lists common mistakes, tips on publicizing the page, and techniques for increasing Web traffic once the site is up and running.

XOOM

http://xoom.com/home/

This is another community-based provider of free Web space. Students and adults who agree to the conditions described on the website can obtain unlimited space to build a personal website and get free building tools.

Yahoo! GeoCities

http://www.geocities.com/join/freehp.html

One of the oldest and biggest names in free Web space, GeoCities offers 11MB of space for development of a personal site, plus free technical support, provided the applicant is willing to abide by the conditions described in the website.

Yet Another "HTCYOHP" (How to Create Your Own Homepage)

http://www.intergalact.com/hp/hp.html

A simple, yet effective tutorial with clear and easy-to-understand instructions for teens on creating their own site. It contains sections on advanced HTML programming, CGI programming, and JAVA. This will enable the most ambitious teens to become super savvy programmers. Written by Sky Coyote, a computer scientist.

Writers & Writing

Try to be Shakespeare. Leave the rest to fate.
– Robert Browning

Creative Writing for Kids Chat

http://kidswriting.miningco.com/

An awesome website for young writers. It contains all sorts of innovative activities and ideas for beginning writers—how to create characters, help with composition, details for stories, character names, historical facts, and ideas for teaching writing to others. A bulletin board, a chat room and a newsletter will keep your teen in contact with other aspiring writers.

Cyber English

http://199.233.193.1/cybereng/

Based on a "learning by doing" pedegogy, CyberEnglish provides a complete online publishing tool, an interactive English course, essays and research on telementoring and mixed media education, and

more. Other features include links to e-text libraries and archives, resources for teachers and writers, and to collaborative sites in Japan, Israel and Spain.

The English Pages!

http://longman.awl.com/englishpages/

Offering free, original materials for instruction in composition, technical writing, basic language arts and internet skills, the English Pages consists of an online citation guide (for properly citing electronic resources), a guide to finding subjects and executing compositions, annotated links for literary research, Internet and literacy exercises, and more.

The English Zone

http://www.glen-net.ca/english/thezone.html

Maintained by a secondary school teacher in Ontario, The English Zone offers help to English teachers and students in researching and writing term papers on such perennial novels as *To Kill a Mockingbird* and *Lord of the Flies*, and on classic plays by Shakespeare and Arthur Miller. It also offers free publication of student poetry.

Inkspot: For Young Writers

http://www.inkspot.com/young

This site highlights useful resources and tips for young writers. It includes practical advice and articles useful to young writers, interviews with professionals in different genres as well as talented young writers, links to network with other young writers, information on online and offline writing groups, associations, and workshops.

Mirror Drive Thru

http://www.mirrormirror.com/

This is another example of a monthly cybermagazine published for and by teens. It includes articles, essays, advice, music/Web reviews, calendars of events interesting to teens, links to writing clubs and related resources.

OneLook Dictionaries, The Faster Finder

http://www.onelook.com

Four hundred and nineteen different dictionaries can be accessed at this single site. It is a handy one stop shopping center for every writer's dictionary needs. Users can search the Internet for a word or acronym or check the spelling of an unusual word. OneLook also offers a Best Price Search. Users can choose a category, like electronics, books, CD's, sports, or movies and learn where to find the best price for the product. Sponsored by Robert K. Ware.

Poetry Today Online

http://www.poetrytodayonline.com/TeenPoetry.html

In addition to offering an opportunity for teens to publish their own poetry online, this site offers young poets an opportunity to share interests through a chat room, and link with other teen poetry clubs and organizations. There are also links to poetry resources such as rhyming dictionaries. This is another excellent example of a publication for teen by teens.

The Quill Society

http://www.quill.net

The Quill Society is an online writing club dedicated to young writers between the ages of 12 and 24. Membership in the club allows contacts with other young writers throughout the world. Opportunities are provided for publication, and critiques of student writing are available. Interviews of successful writers are regularly posted on the site, and members have access to the organization's resource library.

Shadow Magazine

http://www.metro.net/shadow/

Shadow Magazine promotes "exciting fiction for teenagers." Shadow was created to provide teenagers with exceptional literature. Originally produced as a quarterly magazine, the format was changed to an annual to better fit the needs of the readers and producers.

TeenInk

http://www.teenpaper.org/

TeenInk is the online version of the *21st Century*, a 48-page monthly magazine written by teens for teenagers since 1989. Over one million copies are mailed annually mailed high schools and middle/junior highs. The paper is published for young adults by the Young Authors Foundation. Any student can submit articles for this magazine. TeenInk is a condensed version of the print edition, but it includes nonfiction, poetry, fiction, book reviews, movie reviews, college essays, interviews, art and photography, sports, the environment, community service, feedback, and letters to the editor.

Teen World

http://www.teenzworld.com/index_main.htm

This is a general all-around fun site for teens. It features chat, news, contests, e-board, advice, friends, music, movies, books, and games. In the Trivia Blitz section, teens can test their brain power. Teens can also subscribe to the weekly FREE puzzle delivered to their e-mail address. They can play board, strategy, logic and word games, or read about the music world, post and read reviews and meet other music lovers!

Teen Writer's Network

http://www.geocities.com/Heartland/4141

As the teen webmaster of this site says "This is the place to be if you're a person between the ages of 12 and 19 who loves to write. The Tips for New Writers section will help dispel inaccurate notions about the writing process. The Teen Writers Network Idea Center "helps beginners to open the gate to the writer inside them" by listing a selection of really good scenarios as "story starters."

The Twisted Quill

http://members.aol.com/twistquill/home.htm

Help encourage new writers by introducing them to this online young writer's forum. Here budding and accomplished writers can submit their own pieces, read work from other young writers, browse links to the literary giants and their writings, and even gain access to useful education-related websites. Sponsored by Saint Brendan High School.

Vocabulary.com

http://www.vocabulary.com/

With hip cartoon graphics and an enormous archive of interactive games and puzzles, this site simultaneously entertains and helps develop word and language skills. Word games are divided into three skill level categories; regular features include themed comic strips and other word games, and links to thousands of participating schools from around the world.

WWW High School English Resources

http://www.bham.wednet.edu/ENGLISH2.HTM

With links to online style guides, reference archives, and anthologies of American, British, and general literature, this site is the perfect digital assistant for high school students preparing an English/Literature report. Respected authorities and sources like the Rensselaer Writing Center, Columbia University's Bartleby Library, and Orwell's "Politics and the English Language" are all represented.

Wave

http://www.wavemag.com/

A well designed, easy-to-navigate e-zine devoted to teens and writing. Updated monthly, this magazine is chock full of short stories, poems, and essays written by teens as well as a message board and chat room. A great way for teens to see their work published.

Appendix A

Netiquette

Minding Your Manners on the WWW

Netiquette is a combination of the words net and etiquette. It describes the rules for appropriate online behavior. Netiquette is really no different than the rules of decency that should guide our actions no matter where we are.

- Treat others as you would like to be treated.

- Do not give out any personal information about yourself.

- Do not misrepresent yourself or others.

- Do not cheat, steal or do anything you would not like done to yourself.

- Do not plagiarize another's words or ideas.

- Since you may be communicating with someone who lives in another nation, respect other cultures, languages and manners.

- Do not use ALL CAPS. IT LOOKS LIKE YOU ARE SHOUTING!

Appendix B

Safety in Cyberspace

Rules for Online Safety can be boiled down to very simple and memorable concepts:

- Never give out personal information like name, address, phone number, school, places you go, and when you do things.

- Never make plans to meet anyone in person you met online.

- Never tell anyone your password. Anyone who knows your password can access your address, read all of your mail, and generally create havoc with your account.

- Report any bad or suspicious experiences to your Internet service provider.

- Remember that it is easy for people to pretend to be different people online. You really have absolutely no idea with whom you are talking or writing. Even if you have been communicating for awhile, you still have no assurance the persons are who they say they are.

- If you come across a website with "bad" stuff, just click the back button and go somewhere else.

Appendix C

College URLs

Abilene Christian University
Adelphi University
Agnes Scott College
Air Force Institute of Technology
Alabama A& M University
Alabama State University
Alaska Pacific University <www.alaska.net/~apu/>
Albertson College of Idaho
Albion College
Alderson-Broaddus College <www.mountain.net/ab>
Alfred University
Allegheny College
Allentown College of St Francis deSales
Alma College
Ambassador University
American Coastline University
    <www.infotechservices.com/amercst.htm>
American Grad. Sch. of Int'l. Mngt.
American University
Amherst College
Andrews University
Angelo State University
Antioch College
Antioch New England
Antioch University-Los Angeles
    <www.antiochla.edu:7901/>
Antioch University-Seattle
Appalachian State University
Arizona State University
Arizona State University East <www.asu.edu/east/>
Arizona State University West
Arizona Western College
Arkansas State University Jonesboro
Armstrong State College
Ashland University
Assumption College
Athens State College <iquest.com/~athens/>
Auburn University
Auburn University,Montgomery
Augsburg College
Augustana College (IL)

Augustana College (SD)
Aurora University
Austin College
Austin Peay State University
Averett College
Avila College
Azusa Pacific University

Babson College
Baldwin-Wallace College
Ball State University
Baker University
Baptist Bible College
Bard College
Barry University
Bastyr University
Bates College
Baylor College of Medicine
Baylor University
Beaver College
Belmont University <acklen.belmont.edu/welcome.html>
Beloit College
Bemidji State University
Benedictine College
Bennington College
Bentley College
Berea College
Berklee College of Music
Bethany College (CA)
Bethany College (WV)
Bethel College(KS)
Bethel College and Seminary(MN)
Biola University
Birmingham-Southern College
Black Hills State University
Bloomsburg University of Pennsylvania
Bluffton College
Bob Jones University
Boise State University
Boston College
Boston Grad. Sch. of Psychoanalysis

Boston University
Bowdoin College
Bowie State University
Bowling Green State University
Bradley University
Brandeis University
Brenau University
Briar Cliff College
Bridgewater College
Brigham Young University
Brigham Young University Hawaii
Brown University
Bryant College
Bryn Mawr College <www.brynmawr.edu/college>
Bucknell University
Buena Vista University
Butler University

California CoastUniversity
    <www.calcoastuniv.edu/ccu/>
California Institute of Technology
California Lutheran University
California Maritime Academy
California National University
Calif. Polytechnic State Univ., San Luis Obispo
Calif. State Polytechnic Univ., Pomona
California State University System
California State University, Bakersfield
California State University, Chico
California State Univ., Dominguez Hills
California State University, Fresno
California State University, Fullerton
California State University, Hayward
California State University, Long Beach
California State University, Los Angeles
California State Univ., Monterey Bay
California State University, Northridge
California State University, Sacramento
California State Univ., San Bernardino
California State University, San Jose

California State University, San Marcos
California State University, Sacramento
California State University, Stanislaus
California University of Pennsylvania
Calvin College
Campbell University
Campbellsville College
Cameron University
Canisius College
Carleton College
Carnegie Mellon University
Carroll College
Carson-Newman College
Carthage College
Case Western Reserve University
Castleton State University
The Catholic University of America
Cedarville College
Centenary College of Louisiana
Central College
Central Connecticut State UniversityCentral Methodist College
Central Michigan University
Central Missouri State University
Central Washington University
Centre College
Chadron State College
Champlain College
Chapman University
Chatham College
Chesapeake College
Cheyney University
Christian Brothers University
Christian Theological Seminary
Christopher Newport University
The Citadel
City University
City University of New York
Claremont Graduate School
Claremont McKenna College
Clarion University of Pennsylvania
Clark University
Clarke College
Clarkson University
Clemson University <www.clemson.edu/home.html>
Cleveland State University
Clinch Valley College
Coe College
Colby College

Colgate University
College of the Atlantic
College of Charleston
College of Eastern Utah
College of the Holy Cross
College of Saint Benedict
College of Saint Catherine
College of Saint Rose
College of St. Scholastica
College of William and Mary
The College of Wooster
Colorado Christian University
Colorado College
Colorado School of Mines
Colorado State University
Columbia College Chicago
Columbia Southern University
Columbia Union College
Columbia University
Concordia College-Ann Arbor
Concordia College-Moorhead < www.cord.edu/>
Concordia College-St. Paul
Concordia College-Seward
Concordia University River Forest, IL
    <www/curf/home.html>
Connecticut College
The Cooper Union
Cornell College
Cornell University
Cornerstone College <www.grfn.org/~cstone/>
Creighton University

Daemen College
Dakota State University
Dakota Wesleyan University
Dallas Baptist University
Dana College
Daniel Webster College
Dartmouth College
Davenport College
Davidson College
Delaware State University
Delta State University
Denison University
DePaul University
DePauw University
DeVry Institute of Technology
Dickinson College
Dickinson State University
Dillard University
Dominican College

Dordt College
Dowling College
Drake University
Drew University
Drexel University
Duke University
Duquesne University

Earlham College
East Carolina University
East Central University
East Stroudsburg State Univ. of PA
East Tennessee State University
Eastern Connecticut State
Eastern Illinois University
Eastern Kentucky University
Eastern Mennonite University
Eastern Michigan University
Eastern Nazarene College
    <jcrnt.mgh.harvard.edu/enc/enc.htm>
Eastern New Mexico University
Eastern Washington University
Edgewood College
Edinboro University of Pennsylvania
Elizabeth City State University
Elizabethtown College
Elmhurst College
Elon College
Embry-Riddle Aeronautical Univ., AZ
Embry-Riddle Aeronautical Univ., FL
Emerson College
Emmanuel College
Emmaus Bible College
Emporia State University
Emory & Henry CollegeEmory University <www.cc.emory.edu/welcome.html>
Evergreen State College

Fairfield University <192.160.243.26/fairnet1.htm>
Fairleigh Dickinson University
Fairmont State College <www.fairmont.wvnet.edu:80/>
Fayetteville State University
Ferris State University <about.ferris.edu/homepage.htm>
Fisk University
Florida Agricultural & Mechanical Univ.
Florida Atlantic University

Florida Gulf Coast University <www.fgcu.edu/>
Florida Institute of Technology <www.fit.edu/>
Florida International University <www.fiu.edu/>
Florida State University <www.fsu.edu/>
Fontbonne College <www.fontbonne.edu/>
Fordham University <www.fordham.edu/>
Fort Hays State University <www.fhsu.edu/>
Fort Lewis College <www.fortlewis.edu/>
Franciscan University <esoptron.umd.edu/
    FUSFOLDER/>
Franklin and Marshall College <www.fandm.edu/>
Franklin Pierce Law Center <www.fplc.edu/>
Friends University <www.friends.edu/>
Frostburg State University <www.fsu.umd.edu/>
Fuller Theological Seminary <www.fuller.edu/>
Furman University <www.furman.edu/>

George Fox College <www.gfc.edu/>
George Mason University <www.gmu.edu/>
George Washington University <gwis.circ.gwu.edu/>
Georgetown University <www.georgetown.edu/>
Georgia Institute of Technology
    <www.gatech.edu/TechHome.html>
Georgia Military College <www.gmc.cc.ga.us>
Georgia Southern University <www.gasou.edu/>
Georgia Southwestern College
    <gswrs6k1.gsw.peachnet.edu>
Georgia State University <www.gsu.edu/>
Georgian College of Applied Arts and Technology
    <www.georcoll.on.ca/>
Gettysburg College <www.gettysburg.edu>
Goddard College <sun.goddard.edu/>
Golden Gate University <www.ggu.edu/>
Golden West College <www.gwc.cccd.edu/>
Gooding Institute of Nurse Anesthesia
    <www.beaches.net/~gooding>
Gordon College <www.gordonc.edu/>
Gordon-Conwell Theological Seminary <www.gcts.edu>
Goshen College <www.goshen.edu>
Goucher College <www.goucher.edu>
Grace College <www.grace.edu>
Graceland College <www.graceland.edu>
Graduate Institute of International Studies
    <heiwww.unige.ch>
Graduate School, USDA <grad.usda.gov>
Grand Rapids Baptist Seminary
    <www.grfn.org/~cstone/GRBS/GRBS.html>
Grand Valley State University <www.gvsu.edu>
Grant MacEwan Community College <www.gmcc.ab.ca>
Grays Harbor Community College <compbert.ctc.edu>
Grayson County College <grayson.edu>
Graz University of Technology <www.tu-graz.ac.at>
Green Mountain College <www.clanprescott.com/gree-
    nenglish>

Greenville Technical College <www.gvltec.edu>
Griffith University <www.gu.edu.au>
Grinnell College <www.grin.edu>
Grossmont Community College
    <www.gcccd.cc.ca.us/grossmont>
Grove City College
    <www.metronet.com/~rshay/gcc.html>
Guilford Technical Community College
    <technet.gtcc.cc.nc.us>
Gulf Coast Community College <www.gc.cc.fl.us>
Gwynedd Mercy College <www.gmc.edu>

Hahnemann University <www.hahnemann.edu>
Hamilton College <www.hamilton.edu>
Hanover College <www.hanover.edu
Harbin Institute of Technology <202.118.224.101>
Harding University <www.harding.edu>
Hartland Institute of Health and Education <www.hart-
    land.edu/>
Harvard Graduate School of Education <gseweb.har-
    vard.edu>
Harvard University <www.harvard.edu>
Harvey Mudd College <www.hmc.edu>
Hastings College <www.hastings.edu>
Hastings College of Law <www.uchastings.edu>
Haverford College <www.haverford.edu>
Hawaii Pacific University <www.hpu.edu>
Henderson State University <www.hsu.edu>
Hendrix College <192.131.98.11/>
High Point University <www.highpoint.edu>
Higher Colleges of Technology <www.hct.ac.ae>
Hill College <hillcollege.hill-college.cc.tx.us>
Hillsdale College <www.hillsdale.edu>
Hiram College <admission.hiram.edu
Hobart and William Smith Colleges
    <hws3.hws.edu:9000>
Hofstra University <www.hofstra.edu>
Holyoke Community College
    <www.hcc.mass.edu/home.html>
Honolulu Community College <www.hcc.hawaii.edu>
Hood College <www.hood.edu/>
Hope College <www.hope.edu>
Houghton College <www.houghton.edu/>
Houston Community College System
    <www.hccs.cc.tx.us/>
Howard Community College <www.howardcc.edu/>
Howard University <www.howard.edu>
Hudson Valley Community College <www.hvcc.edu>
Humboldt State University <www.humboldt.edu>
Huntingdon College <www.huntingdon.edu>

Idaho State University <www.isu.edu>
Illinois Benedictine College <www.ibc.edu/>
Illinois College <www.ic.edu/>
Illinois Institute of Technology <www.iit.edu/>
Illinois State University <www.ilstu.edu/>

Illinois Wesleyan University <www.iwu.edu/>
Indiana State University <www-isu.indstate.edu/>
Indiana University <www.indiana.edu/>
Indiana University South Bend <www.iusb.edu/>
Indiana University Southeast <www.ius.indiana.edu>
Indiana University of Pennsylvania <www.lib.iup.edu/>
Indiana University, Bloomington
    <www.indiana.edu/iub/>
Indiana Wesleyan University <www.indwes.edu/>
Institute of Clinical Pharmacology and Toxicology
    <www.uniud.it/ifct>
Iowa State University <www.iastate.edu>
Ithaca College <www.ithaca.edu>

Jackson State Community College
    <erc.jscc.cc.tn.us/jscc.html>
Jackson State University <www.jsums.edu/>
Jacksonville State University
    <jsucc.jsu.edu/welcome.html>
Jacksonville State University, Alabama <www.jsu.edu/>
Jacksonville University <junix.ju.edu>
James Cook University <www.jcu.edu.au/>
James Madison University <www.jmu.edu/>
Jamestown College <acc.jc.edu/>
Jefferson State Community College
    <www.quicklink.net/bham/jscc/>
John Brown University <www.jbu.edu/>
Carroll University <www.jcu.edu/>
John F. Kennedy School of Government <ksgwww.harvard.edu/>
John Marshall Law School <www.jmls.edu/>
Johns Hopkins University <www.jhu.edu/>
Johnson & Wales University, Rhode Island
    <www.jwu.edu>
Johnson & Wales University, South Carolina
    <www.sims.net/organizations/jwu-sc/jwu.html>
Johnson C. Smith University <www.jcsu.edu>
Johnson County Community College
    <www.johnco.cc.ks.us/docs/Welcome.html>
Joliet Junior College <ac4.jjc.cc.il.us>
Jones College <www.jones.edu>
Jones County Junior College <www.jcjc.cc.ms.us>
Judson College <www.judson-il.edu>

Kalamazoo College <kzoo.edu>
Kansas State University <www.ksu.edu>

La Salle University <www.lasalle.edu/home.html>
La Sierra University <www.lasierra.edu>
LaGrange College <www.lgc.peachnet.edu>
LaSalle College Group <www.clasalle.qc.ca>
Lafayette College <www.lafayette.edu>
Lake Forest College <www.lfc.edu>
Lake Superior College <www.lsc.cc.mn.us>
Lake Superior State University <www.lssu.edu>

Langston University <www.lunet.edu>
Le Moyne College <shttp://www.lemoyne.edu>
Lebanon Valley College <www.lvc.edu>
Lehigh Carbon Community College
    <lib3.lccc.edu/library.html>
Lehigh University <www.lehigh.edu>
Lincoln University <www.lincoln.ac.nz>
Lincoln University of Pennsylvania <www.lincoln.edu>
Lock Haven University of Pennsylvania <www.lhup.edu>
Logan College of Chiropractic <www.logan.edu>
Loma Linda University <www.llu.edu>
Long Island University <www.liunet.edu>
Longview Community College
    <www.longview.cc.mo.us>
Longwood College <www.lwc.edu>
Los Angeles Community Colleges <www.laccd.edu>
Los Angeles Harbor College
    <edweb.sdsu.edu/lahc/homepage.htm>
Louisiana State University <unix1.sncc.lsu.edu>
Louisiana State University Medical Center
    <www.lsumc.edu>
Louisiana State University, Shreveport <www.lsus.edu>
Louisiana Tech University <aurora.latech.edu>
Lousiana College <www.lacollege.edu>
Loyola College <www.loyola.edu>
Loyola Marymount University <www.lmu.edu>
Loyola University, Chicago <www.luc.edu>
Loyola University, New Orleans <www.loyno.edu>
Lycoming College <www.lycoming.edu>
Lynchburg College <www.lynchburg.edu>
Lynn University <www.lynn.edu>

Macalester College <www.macalstr.edu/>
Maharishi University of Management <www.mum.edu/>
Maine Maritime Academy <www.state.me.us/
    maritime/mma.htm>
Malone College <www.malone.edu/>
Manhattan College <www.mancol.edu/>
Mankato State University <www.mankato.msus.edu/>
Mansfield University of Pennsylvania <www.mnsfld.edu/>
Marietta College <www.marietta.edu/>
Marist College <www.marist.edu/>
Marlboro College <www.marlboro.edu/>
Marquette University <www.mu.edu/>
Marshall University <www.marshall.edu/>
Mary Baldwin College <www.mbc.edu/>
Maryland College of Art and Design
    <writer.org/mcac/mcad/main.htm>
Marymount College <www.marymt.edu/>
Marymount University <www.marymount.edu/>
Mary Washington College <www.mwc.edu/>
Massachusetts Institute of Technology <web.mit.edu/>
McMurray University <www.mcm.acu.edu/>
McNeese State University <www.mcneese.edu/>

Medical College of Georgia
Medical College of Wisconsin
Mercer University
Mercyhurst College
Meredith College <www.meredith.edu/meredith/>
Messiah College
Metropolitan State College of Denver
Metropolitan State University
Miami Christian University
Miami University of Ohio
Michigan State University
Michigan Technological University
Mid-America Nazarene College
Middlebury College
Middle Tennessee State University
Midwestern State University
Millersville University of Pennsylvania
Milligan College
Millikin University
Millsaps College
Milwaukee School of Engineering
Minot State University
Minneapolis College of Art and Design
Mississippi College
Mississippi State University
Mississippi University for Women
Missouri Southern State College
Missouri Western State College
Molloy College
Monmouth College
Monmouth University
Montana State University-Billings
Montana State University-Bozeman
Montana State University-Northern
Montana Tech
Montclair State University
Montreat College
Moravian College
Moorhead State University
Morehouse College <144.125.128.1:1025/>
Morgan State University
Mount Holyoke College
Mount Saint Joseph College
Mount Saint Mary College
Mount Union College
Murray State University
Muskingum College

National Defense University
National-Louis University
National Technological University
National University
Naval Postgraduate School
Nazareth College
Newberry College
New England Institute of Technology <media1.hyper-
     net.com/neit.html>
New College of California
New Hampshire College
New Jersey Institute of Technology
New Mexico Highlands University
New Mexico Institute of Mining & Tech.
New Mexico State University
New York Institute of Technology
New York University
Niagara University
Nicholls State University
Norfolk State University
North Carolina A&T State University
North Carolina State University
North Central Bible College
North Dakota State University
North Park College & Theological Sem.
Northeast Missouri StateUniversity
Northeastern Louisiana University
Northeastern State University
Northeastern University
Northern Arizona University
Northern Illinois University
Northern Kentucky University
Northern Michigan University
Northern State University
Northwest Missouri State University
Northwest Nazarene College
Northwestern College of Iowa
Northwestern State University
Northwestern University
Norwich University
Nova Southeastern University

Oakland University
Oberlin College
Occidental College
Ohio Dominican College
Ohio Northern University

Ohio State University, Columbus
Ohio State University, Marion
Ohio Wesleyan University
Ohio University, Athens
Oklahoma Baptist University
Oklahoma City University
Oklahoma State University
Old Dominion University
Olivet Nazarene University
Oral Roberts University
Oregon Grad. Institute of Sci. & Tech. <www.ogi.edu/welcome.html>
Oregon Health Sciences University
Oregon Institute of Technology
Oregon State University
Otterbein College
Our Lady of the Lake University

Pace University
Pacific Lutheran University
Pacific Union College
Pacific Western University
Peace College
Pembroke State University
Pennsylvania State Sys. of Higher Ed. <sshe2.sshechan.edu/sshe.html>
Pennsylvania State University
Pennsylvania State Univ. – Schuylkill
Pensacola Christian College
Pepperdine University
Peru State College
Pittsburg State University
Pitzer College
Platt College
Plymouth State College
Point Loma Nazarene College <192.147.249.89/>
Polytechnic University of New York
Polytechnic University of Puerto Rico
Pomona College
Portland State University
Prairie View A&M University
Pratt Institute
Princeton University
Presbyterian College
Providence College
Purdue University
Purdue University Calumet
Purdue University North Central

Quincy University

Radford University
Ramapo College
Randolph-Macon College
Randolph-Macon Woman's College
Reed College
Regent University
Regis University
Rensselaer Polytechnic Institute
Rhode Island College
Rhodes College
Rice University
Richard Stockton College of NJ
Rider University
Ripon College <WWW.Ripon.edu/>
Rivier College
Roanoke College
Rochester Institute of Technology
The Rockefeller University
Rockford College
Rockhurst College
Rocky Mountain College
Roger Williams University
Rollins College
Rosary College
Rose-Hulman Institute of Technology
Rowan College
Rutgers University
Rutgers University, Camden
Rutgers University, Newark <www.rutgers.edu/newark/>

Sage Colleges
Sacred Heart University
Saginaw Valley State University
St. Ambrose University <www.sau.edu/sau.html>
Saint Anselm College
St. Bonaventure University
Saint Cloud State University
Saint Edward's University <www.stedwards.edu/home.htm>
Saint Francis College
St. John's College – Annapolis <www.sjca.edu/main.html>
St. John's College – Santa Fe
Saint John's University (MN)
Saint John's University (NY)
St. Joseph College (CT)

Saint Joseph's College (IN)

St. Joseph's College (ME)

Saint Joseph's University

St. Lawrence University

St. Louis College of Pharmacy

Saint Louis University

St. Martin's College

Saint Mary's College (IN)

Saint Mary's College of California

Saint Mary's University of Minnesota

Saint Michael's College

Saint Olaf College

St. Thomas University (FL)

Saint Vincent College

Saint Xavier University

Salisbury State University

Salish Kootenai College

Sam Houston State University

Samford University

San Diego State University

San Francisco State University

San Jose State University

Santa Clara University

Sarah Lawrence College

School of the Art Institute of Chicago <www.artic.edu/saic/saichome.html/>

Seattle Pacific University

Seattle University

Seton Hall University

Sewanee, University of the South

Shawnee State University

Shenandoah University

Shippensburg University of PA

Simmons College

Simon's Rock College

Simpson College

Skidmore College

Slippery Rock University of PA

Smith College

Sonoma State University

South Dakota School of Mines & Tech.

South Dakota State University

Southeast Missouri State University

Southeastern Louisiana University

Southern College

Southern College of Technology

Southern Connecticut State University

Southern Illinois University

Southern Illinois University – Carbondale cwis/>

Southern Illinois University-Edwardsville

Southern Methodist University

Southern Nazarene University

Southern Oregon State College

Southern University

Southern Utah University

Southampton College

Southwest Baptist University

Southwest Missouri State University

Southwest State University

Southwest Texas State University

Southwestern Adventist College

Southwestern University

Spellman College

Spring Arbor College

Spring Hill College

Stanford University

SUNY System

SUNY at Albany <cscmosaic.albany.edu/home.html>

SUNY at Binghamton

SUNY at Buffalo

SUNY at Fredonia

SUNY at Oswego

SUNY at Plattsburgh

SUNY at Stony Brook

SUNY College of Tech. at Alfred

SUNY College at Brockport

SUNY College of A&M at Cobleskill

SUNY College at Cortland

SUNY College of Envt. Sci. & Forestry

SUNY College at Geneseo

SUNY College at New Paltz

SUNY College at Oneonta <137.141.153.38/>

SUNY College at Potsdam <www.potsdam.edu/PotsdamHome.html>

SUNY Institute of Tech. at Utica/Rome

Stephen F. Austin State University

Stephens College

Stetson University

Stevens Institute of Technology

Strayer College

Suffolk University

Sul Ross State University

Susquehanna University

Swarthmore College

Sweet Briar College
Syracuse University

Tabor College
Tarleton State University
Taylor University
Teachers College
Teikyo Marycrest University
Temple University
Tennessee State University
Tennessee Technological University
Texas A&M International University
Texas A&M University-College Station
Texas A&M University-Corpus Christi
Texas A&M University-Kingsville
Texas Christian University
Texas Southern University
Texas Tech University
Texas Tech Univ.-Health Sciences Ctr.
Texas Woman's University
Thomas College
Thomas Edison State College
Thomas Jefferson University
Thomas More College
Towson State University
Transylvania University
Trenton State College
Trinity College (CT)
    <www.trincoll.edu/homepage.html>
Trinity College
    <www.consortium.org/~trinity/home.htm>
Trinity University
Troy State University
Tucson University
Tufts University
Tulane University
Tuskegee University

Union College
Union University
United States Air Force Academy
United States Merchant Marine Acad.
United States Military Academy
United States Naval Academy
Uniformed Svcs. Univ. of Health Sci.
Ursinus College
University of Akron

University of Alabama at Birmingham
University of Alabama at Huntsville
University of Alabama at Tuscaloosa
University of Alaska
University of Alaska-Fairbanks
    <info.alaska.edu:70/1s/UA/UA_Fairbanks>
University of Alaska-Southeast
University of Arizona
University of Arkansas – Fayetteville
University of Arkansas – Little Rock
University of Arkansas for Medical Science
University of Arkansas – Monticello
University of Baltimore
University of Bridgeport
University of California, Berkeley
University of California, Davis
University of California, Irvine
University of California, Los Angeles
University of California, Riverside
University of California, San Diego
University of California, San Francisco
University of California, Santa Barbara
University of California, Santa Cruz
University of Central Arkansas
University of Central Florida
University of Charleston
University of Chicago
University of Cincinnati
University of Colorado at Boulder
University of Colorado at CO Springs
University of Colorado at Denver
Univ. of CO Health Sciences CenterUniversity of Connecticut
University of Dallas
University of Dayton
University of Delaware
University of Denver
University of Detroit Mercy
University of Dubuque
University of Evansville
University of Florida
University of Georgia
University of Guam
University of Hartford
    <www.hartford.edu/UofHWelcome.html>
Univ. of Hawaii at Hilo Physics & Astrny
University of Hawaii at Manoa <www.hawaii.edu/uhin-
    fo.html>

University of Houston
University of Idaho
University of Illinois at Chicago
University of Illinois at Springfield
University of IL at Urbana-Champaign
University of Indianapolis
University of Iowa
University of Kansas
    cwis/UDK/KUhome/KUHo
    me.html>
University of Kansas Sch. of Medicine
University of Kentucky
University of Louisville
University of Maine System
University of Maine
University of Maine at Farmington
University of Maine at Fort Kent
University of Maine at Machias
University of Maine at Presque Island
University of Maryland at Baltimore
University of Maryland at Baltimore Co.
University of Maryland at College Park
University of Maryland – Univ. College
University of Massachusetts System
University of Massachusetts at Amherst
Univ. of Massachusetts at Dartmouth
University of Massachusetts at Lowell
University of Memphis
University of Miami
University of Michigan-Ann Arbor
University of Michigan – Dearborn
University of Minnesota
University of Minnesota – Crookston
University of Minnesota – Duluth
University of Minnesota – Morris
University of Minnesota – Twin Cities
    <www.tc.umn.edu/tc/>
University of Mississippi
University of Mississippi Medical Center

University of Missouri System
University of Missouri – Columbia
University of Missouri – Kansas City
University of Missouri – Rolla
University of Missouri – Saint Louis
University of Montana
University of Nebraska, Kearney
University of Nebraska, Lincoln
University of Nebraska, Omaha
University of Nevada, Las Vegas
University of Nevada, Reno <www.scs.unr.edu/unr/>
University of New England
University of New Hampshire, Durham
University of New Haven
University of New Mexico
University of New Orleans
University of North Carolina at Asheville
University of North Carolina at Chapel Hill
University of North Carolina at Charlotte
University of North Carolina at Greensboro
University of North Carolina System
Univ. of North Carolina at Wilmington
University of North Dakota
University of North Florida
University of North Texas
University of Northern Colorado
University of Northern Iowa
University of Notre Dame
University of Oklahoma
University of Oregon
University of the Ozarks
University of the Pacific
University of Pennsylvania
University of Phoenix
University of Pittsburgh
University of Pittsburgh at Johnstown
    <www.pitt.edu/~upjweb>
University of Portland
University of Puerto Rico
    <www.upr.clu.edu/home.html>
University of Puget Sound
University of Redlands
University of Rhode Island
University of Richmond

University of Rochester
University of San Diego
University of San Francisco
University of Sarasota <www.sol.sarasota.fl.us/univ.html>
University of Science & Arts of OK
University of Scranton
University of Sioux Falls
University of Southern California
University of South Carolina
University of South Carolina – Aiken
University of South Dakota
University of South Florida
University of Southern Maine
University of Southern Mississippi
University of Southwestern Louisiana
University of Saint Thomas
University of Saint Thomas (MN)
University of South Alabama
University of Southern Colorado
University of Southern Indiana
University of Tennessee, Knoxville
University of Tennessee, Martin
University of Texas System
University of Texas at Arlington
University of Texas at Austin
University of Texas at Brownsville
University of Texas at Dallas
University of Texas at El Paso
University of Texas-Pan AmericanUniversity of Texas at San Antonio
Univ. of TX Health Sci. Ctr. at Houston
Univ. of TX Health Sci. Ctr. – SanAntonioUniversity of Texas at Tyler <192.88.13.33/>
Univ. of Texas Health Center at Tyler
    <pegasus.uthct.edu/UTHCT-Home/Welcome.html>
Univ. of TX M.D. Anderson Cancer Ctr.
University of Texas Medical Branch
Univ. of TX SW Med. Ctr. at Dallas
University of Toledo
University of Tulsa
University of Utah
    <www.utah.edu/HTML_Docs/UofU_Home.html>
University of Vermont
University of the Virgin Islands
University of Virginia, Charlottesville
University of Washington

University of West Alabama
University of West Florida
University of Wisconsin System
University of Wisconsin – Eau Claire
University of Wisconsin – Green Bay
University of Wisconsin – LaCrosse
University of Wisconsin – Madison
University of Wisconsin – Milwaukee
University of Wisconsin – Oshkosh
University of Wisconsin – Parkside
University of Wisconsin – Platteville
University of Wisconsin – River Falls
University of Wisconsin – Stevens Point
University of Wisconsin – Stout
University of Wisconsin – Superior
University of Wisconsin – Whitewater
University of Wyoming
Upper Iowa University
Utah State University
Utah Valley State College

Valley City State University
    <www.vcsu.nodak.edu/home.html>
Valdosta State University
Valparaiso University
Vanderbilt University
Vassar College
Vermont Technical College
Villa Julie College
Villanova University
Virginia Commonwealth University
Virginia Military Institute
Virginia Polytechnic Institute
Virginia Wesleyan College

Wabash College
Wake Forest University <www.wfu.edu/www-
    data/start.html>
Walden University
Walla Walla College
Warren Wilson College
Wartburg College
Washburn University
Washington Bible College
Washington & Lee University
Washington College
Washington State University
Washington State Univ. at Tri-Cities
Washington State Univ. at Vancouver

Washington University, Saint Louis
Wayne State University
Waynesburg College
Weber State University
Webster University
Wellesley College
Wells College
Wentworth Institute of Technology
Wesleyan University
West Chester University of PA
West Coast University
West Georgia College
West Liberty State College
West Texas A&M University
West Virginia University
Western Carolina University
Western Connecticut State UniversityWestern Illinois University
Western Kentucky University
Western Maryland College
Western Michigan University
Western Montana College
Western New England College
Western New Mexico University
Western State College
Western Washington University
Westminster College
Westminster College
Westminster College of Salt Lake City
Westminster Theological Seminary

Westmont College
Wheaton College
Wheaton College, Norton MA
Wheeling Jesuit College
Whitman College
Whittier College
Whitworth College
Wichita State University
Widener University
Wilberforce University
Wilkes University
Willamette University
William Jewell College
William Penn College
William Paterson College
William Woods University
Williams College
Wilmington College
Winona State University
Winthrop University <lurch.winthrop.edu/
    WinthropHome Page.html>
Wittenberg University
Wofford College
Worcester Polytechnic Institute
Wright State University

Xavier University of Louisiana

Yale University
Yeshiva University
York College of Pennsylvania
Youngstown State University

Index to Websites

X–Z